The cost
of Europe

The cost of Europe

edited by Patrick Minford

Manchester University Press
Manchester and New York
Distributed exclusively in the USA and Canada by St. Martin's Press

Published by Manchester University Press
Oxford Road, Manchester M13 9PL, UK
and Room 400, 175 Fifth Avenue,
New York, NY 10010, USA

Distributed exclusively in the USA and Canada
by St. Martin's Press, Inc.,
175 Fifth Avenue, New York, NY 10010, USA

British Library Cataloguing-in-Publication Data
A cataloguing record for this book is available from the British Library

Library of Congress Cataloging-in-Publication Data applied for

ISBN 0 7190 3809 X *hardback*
0 7190 3810 3 *paperback*

Printed in Great Britain
by Biddles Ltd, Guildford and King's Lynn

Contents

Foreword
Kenneth Minogue
Professor of Political Science at the LSE
and Chairman of The Bruges Group vii

Preface x

Biographical Notes xi

The Bruges Group xiv

1 Introduction
Patrick Minford 1

Part I What Sort of Political Union?

2 History casts doubts on the Euro-dream
Norman Stone 19

3 The Brussels Leviathan
Alan Walters 24

4 A proposal for monetary union
Alan Sked 30

Part II Fortress Europe

5 The Common Agricultural Policy
Richard Howarth 51

6 Trade Policy of the European Community
Brian Hindley 84

7 Eastern Europe and the EEC
Martin Holmes 102

Part III Unification: evolution or standardisation

8 Britain and the exchange rate mechanism
Alan Walters 119

9 The price of monetary unification
Patrick Minford 125

10 The Social Charter
Ben Roberts 142

Appendix: The effect in the UK of EEC Wage proposals in the social charter
Patrick Minford and Paul Ashton 164

11 Taxation in Britain and Europe in the 1990s
Tim Congdon 173

Foreword

The greatest of all students of politics – I refer, of course, to Aesop – told the story of the wind and the sun competing as to which of them could induce a man to take off his coat. The wind blew, and the more it blew, the more the man pulled his coat tight round him. Then the sun shone, and the coat came off.

This is a suggestive parallel for British experience in the twentieth century. Faced with the hurricane of Hitler in 1940, the British refused to abandon any of the independence which would so temptingly have promised salvation from the threat they faced. Responding to the embrace of Europe in the later part of the century, they have been eager to shed coat, jumper, and in some cases almost everything. The contrast is clearly one between a self-confident nation proud of its history and traditions, and a nation which, in spite of its manifold blessings, has picked up a mood of intellectually fashionable self-doubt.

My parable applies, of course, only to the conduct of the British. There are obviously immense and vital differences between Hitler's new order and the ambitions of the European Community. The question for Britain – and also a question for each nation in the Twelve – is what form our increasing integration with our European neighbours will take. No-one, I think, doubts the importance and the desirability of these developments. The problem is that public opinion is remarkably ignorant of what is involved. That is why *The cost of Europe* is a major contribution to public understanding. It ought to be found invaluable no less by its opponents than by its supporters, partly because it clarifies a flabby public discussion, but above all because it is full of hard information otherwise difficult to come by.

That very fact tells us a lot about the way in which the present institutions of the Community have developed. During 1991 it proved remarkably difficult to get hold of the draft treaties which were to be discussed at Maastricht. I once heard the history of the Community described by one of its founding fathers as a 'benign conspiracy'. It is a description that reveals a lot. Between the grand declarations of intent and the tedious technicality of the fine print, nations often found themselves committed to more than they had bargained for. As Ben Roberts points out, the Single European Act agreed that the unanimity rule would only be modified on grounds of health and safety; the Commission has already attempted to drive a coach and horses called the 'Social Charter' through this concession. The constant changes of name - the EEC, changing insensibly to the European Community, and now the European Union - further conspire to suggest that it is all being done by mirrors.

Such an impression is not helped by evident contradictions in the Community's public position. As Brian Hindley observes: 'M. Delors and other members of the European Commission constantly say that the EEC rejects protectionism. But they also affirm the CAP as a foundation stone of the EEC. The statements cannot be reconciled.' Patrick Minford fittingly describes as coy the term 'social and economic cohesion' which covers, one might almost say covers up, the vastly expensive project of subsidising the poorer countries in order to bring them up to the standard of the richer. And whoever wants to catch the true flavour of special interests protecting themselves by manipulating a bureaucratic apparatus need look no further than the page on which Martin Holmes cites the list of restrictions imposed on Polish trade with the Community.

The essence of the European Community is that it trades in futures. Dangling a vision before the bemused eyes of those looking for a new and more peaceful order, it works, by an adroit mixture of persuasion and intimidation, to acquire ever greater executive power to regulate our lives. Its moral force comes from its promise to transcend the narrow nationalism of the past, but on many issues – ranging from the CAP to taking responsibility in the Gulf War – it has a far less impressive record of international virtue than has Britain and other member states. When flattery and persuasion fail to increase its power at meetings of heads of government, the Commission attempts to isolate and intimidate recalcitrant nations, a tactic all the more effective because in the British case it is echoed in a servile way by some elements of the British press. Everyone, we were often told before the Maastricht conference, was becoming *impatient* with British hesitation. Let time reveal whether the sceptics or the partisans of the Commission were closer to reality. The stakes in this game are certainly grand enough for us to think in historical terms, and everyone involved in this book looks forward to the day when, on issues where we are right, we have the confidence to stand by the old joke: 'Fog in the Channel. Continent isolated.'

Kenneth Minogue

Preface

This book was completed after the Maastricht Treaty was initialled in December 1991. Since then the Danish Referendum rejecting the Treaty has led to widespread questioning of its assumptions. While the Treaty is technically dead, its proponents will undoubtedly make great efforts to revive it. This book will, we hope, inform the debate going on throughout Europe about whether it is worth reviving and if so in what precise form. It is written as if the Treaty could still be ratified as it now stands: that is most unlikely to be the case, but the analysis here applied as strongly to whatever approximation to it its proponents are likely to being forward for consideration over the coming months.

The book is published in association with the Bruges Group, which exists to foster debate about the possible development of the EEC within a free society. I am grateful to the Patrons of the Group for their support and encouragement of this publication and the work that is discussed in it; to Francis Brooke, the chief executive of Manchester University Press, who has ensured that it has appeared with considerable speed; and to Jane Francis and Simon Blackman who coordinated the typsetting within the Department of Economics and Accounting's European Economies Unit at Liverpool University.

Patrick Minford
June 25th 1992

Biographic Notes

Tim Congdon is managing director of the economics consultancy, Lombard Street Research Limited, and economic adviser to the Gerrard and National group. He is honorary professor of economics at Cardiff Business School. His books include *Monetary Control in Britain* (1982), *The Debt Threat* (1988) and *Reflections on Monetarism* (1992, forthcoming).

Brian Hindley is Senior Lecturer in Economics at the London School of Economics and Vice-Chairman of the Bruges Group. His publications include *Europe: Fortress or Freedom*? (Bruges Group, 1989), 'Dumping in the Far East trade of the European Community' (*World Economy*, 1988), and *What Britain pays for Voluntary Export Restraints* (Trade Policy Research Centre, 1985).

Martin Holmes has been Senior Visiting Research Fellow, Mansfield College, Oxford since 1987. He has a degree in P.P.E. from Oxford followed by a doctorate there on the economic policies of the Heath Government (awarded 1981). He is the author of *Yugoslavia and EEC* (Bruges Group, 1990). He lectured in USSR, Poland, Yugoslavia, Albania and Czechoslovakia; and was present in Romania during the 1989 revolution in Timisoara.

Richard W. Howarth is Senior Lecturer in Agricultural Economics in the School of Agricultural and Forest Sciences, University of Wales, Bangor. His main publications include *Farming for Farmers? A Critique of Agricultural Support Policy* (2nd edn) (1990), Institute of Economic affairs, and with Michael Hollingham, *British Milk Market-*

ing and the CAP: Origins of Confusion and Crisis (1989), Avebury. He has acted as an advisor to government departments and many other organisations.

Patrick Minford has been Edward Gonner Professor of Applied Economics, University of Liverpool since 1976. Between 1967 and 1974 he acted as economic adviser to: Finance Director, Courtaulds Limited; Ministry of Finance, Malawi; HM Treasury's external division, and its Delegation in Washington D.C.. He was Hallsworth Fellow, Manchester University, in 1975 and edited the NIESR Review in 1976. Publications include: *Substitution Effects, Speculation and Exchange Rate Stability; Unemployment Cause and Cure; The Housing Morass*; and *Rational Expectations Macroeconomics* (forthcoming). He writes a regular column in *The Daily Telegraph.* Member of Monopolies and Mergers Commission since March 1990.

B.C. Roberts M.A. is Emeritus Professor of Industrial Relations, London University. Founder and Editor of the British Journal of Industrial Relations, 1963-1989. Former President of the British Universities Industrial Relations Association, 1962-1965. First President International Industrial Relations Association, 1964-1973. Member of Council of Advisory Conciliation and Arbitration Service, 1979-1987. Member of National Reference Tribunals for the Mining Industry. Sometime consultant to the ILO, OECD, and the EEC. Publications include: *Trade Unions in a Free Society*, 1959; *The Trades Union congress*, 1868-1921; *National Wages Policy in War and Peace*, 1958; *Industrial Relations in Europe* (ed. 1985); *New Departures in Industrial Relations in the USA, Canada and the United Kingdom* (with G. Lodge and H. Okomoto) 1988.

Dr. Alan Sked is Senior Lecturer in International History at the LSE. From 1981-90 he was also Convener of European Studies there. He is the author of many books and pamphlets on European and British history and politics. His books include *The Decline and Fall of the Habsburg Empire 1815-1918* and *Post-war Britain, a political history.* He is currently writing the Penguin history of post-war Europe and the Macmillan history of nineteenth-century Europe. He is Chairman of the Anti-Federalist League and has written extensively for the Bruges Group.

Norman Stone is Professor of Modern History, University of Oxford. His main publications are *The Eastern Front 1914-17, Europe Transformed 1871-1919* and *The Other Russia, a study of the immigration after 1917*. He is a trustee of the Thatcher Foundation and writes a regular column in the *Sunday Times*.

Alan A. Walters is Vice Chairman of AIG Trading Corporation and a senior fellow at the American Enterprise Institute. He has held a number of academic positions in Great Britian and United States, including professorships at John Hopkins University, the University of Birmingham and the London School of Economics, where he was the Sir Ernest Cassel Professor of Economics. He is a widely published author whose thirteen books include *The Economics of Road User Charges, Money in Boom and Slump, Britain's Economic Renaissance: Margaret Thatcher's Reforms, 1979-1984,* and most recently *Sterling in Danger: The Economic Consequences of Pegged Exchange Rates.* He has been chief economic adviser to Margaret Thatcher, and adviser to the World Bank, various governments, central banks, and financial institutions. He was knighted by Queen Elizabeth II in June 1983.

The Bruges Group

The Bruges Group was set up in early 1989 in order to campaign for a Europe less subject to centralised administrative control than that emerging in Brussels. Its inspiration was Margaret Thatcher's Bruges Speech in which she remarked that Britain had not rolled back the frontiers of the state in order to have them reimposed from Brussels. Lady Thatcher is the patron of the Group. In its early campaigning days it soon had a major effect on public opinion, and forged links with similarly minded members of Parliament, as well as with similarly minded groups in other countries and in the Community. It published pamphlets and monographs, and a book *Reshaping Europe in the Twenty First Century* which was based on a major conference held in London in November 1990. This book was edited by Patrick Robertson, who had originally inspired the Group and became its Secretary during those early years.

Over the last year, other groups with similar interests have arisen, and the Group has evolved in a new and more academic direction. The Group feels strongly that the issue of Europe is the most momentous in current British politics, and that the level of public debate has not responded to this importance. While strongly attached to the tradition of British democracy and sovereignty, members of the Group are basically concerned to ensure that the full complexity of the issues should emerge in public life. To this end, it has set up four high powered working parties - covering political and constitutional issues, economic and financial, social and cultural and defence and foreign policy - whose reports will be among the bases for future meetings of the Group. *The Cost of Europe* brings together facts and analysis which are intended to inform the public debate and to provide a starting point for these working parties' deliberations.

1 *Patrick Minford*

Introduction

In the past few years it has become apparent that a particular plan for Europe was being attempted by the European Commission under Jacques Delors, with the support of a shifting majority of countries, depending on the issue in hand. That plan can be loosely characterised as federalist – with a strong central directing bureaucracy, buttressed by a European central bank controlling a single currency – and corporatist – with strong links between that bureaucracy and major industrial companies in Europe and a social partnership with unions backed up by a 'Social Charter'. The plan is built upon the previous elements in the Rome Treaty and the Single European Act which extended it; but it contradicts some of these elements, notably the commitments to a free internal market competing on level terms with foreign suppliers who would so set a standard of discipline for European industry. Other elements are consistent with it, including the protectionist Common Agricultural Policy (CAP) and the European Court, which has seen its role, in the continental legal tradition, as one of reinforcing bureaucratic actions.

There have been intermittent and partial efforts to evaluate this programme. The EC Commission itself has produced two large volumes, one on the Single Market, the other on the Single Currency. The CAP, longest in being, has spawned a large literature. The Exchange Rate Mechanism of the European Monetary System, the route that is currently supposed to lead to the Single Currency, has also been widely reviewed. But the more recent and the intended future parts have had less independent attention, whether the Single Currency, the federalism or the corporatism.

In this book a group of authors who have written extensively about these plans and previous elements of the European Community have gathered together to consider the current project, in association with the Bruges Group. The Bruges Group is composed of a council of academics; it also has an individual membership in the UK and other European countries. It was founded in order to promote a broad and well-informed public debate over proposals for the future of the EEC; it was named after Mrs Thatcher's famous speech at Bruges on September 20 1988, in which she questioned the federalist, inward-looking vision championed by M. Delors and contrasted it with a Europe committed to free markets and a widening membership, particularly bringing in the new market economies of Eastern Europe. The academic founder-members of the Group share Mrs Thatcher's commitment to free markets and an outward-looking Europe.

The authors of this book are drawn from these and other like-minded academics. All are experts in their fields, and their contributions must be taken with the utmost seriousness. We could also have included chapters by protagonists for the official Delors line; we decided not to, since the EEC has seen to it that such work is prolific, easily available and already gets the widest attention. Besides, to do it justice would have taken up much space in a tightly-organised book. The result is that this book takes a consistently 'Euro-sceptical' line towards many of the official EEC Commission's positions. But in so doing it is intended to bring balance back to a debate that has been dominated by the official line.

Each chapter is devoted to what we see as the key issues concerning the current and future state of Europe. We have tried to be quantitative in these assessments. But naturally this is not always possible. We look at costs and benefits. The intention is to enable the reader to assemble a cost-benefit balance sheet of the present plans being pursued by Jacques Delors. By reviewing alternatives to these plans, we also hope the reader can analyse that balance sheet critically for scope for improvement.

We begin with the political agenda. Norman Stone and Alan Walters set the scene in two short contributions. Norman Stone considers the historical background and notes the contrast between the bureaucratic zeal of the unifiers and the indifference of the vast majority of Europeans, who want efficient co-operation more than anything else. This desire has been exploited by certain groups: Herr Kohl's government for its aim of 'tying down' German nationalism; the Lombards to get shot of the Mezzogiorno; the smaller countries and of course the Commission for more power, and so on. But in the end the people of Europe will have to agree and should be consulted; a UK referendum would set a useful example (the Danes already are bound to have one on each of monetary and political parts of the Maastricht Treaty) and act as a constraint on this exploitation.

Alan Walters considers the broad sweep of the Delors agenda and the cleverness of his overall tactics. He notes that few if any of the peoples of the EEC would want a centralised federal union, given their past histories of independence. Instead, therefore, of proposing this as the principal aim and object of a new treaty, Delors has placed the emphasis on the more technical aim of monetary union. This could be sold to the people and to business as a way of reducing irritating currency barriers to tourism and trade; yet to make it work it would require a powerful central government with a large budget. Centralism and political union would therefore come in by the back door. According to Walters, monetary union is the Trojan Horse bringing in the forces of political union by stealth; and he believes that M. Delors and his allies have been successful in duping the governments and peoples of Europe into welcoming the Horse into their midst, with the inevitable consequences that it will unleash. One must hope that he is too pessimistic about the inevitability of such a process – but it can only be a hope at this stage.

What sort of political union is planned by the Delors group? Plainly it is a federalised centralist set of proposals, according to the original Luxembourg draft; this has now been superseded by the Dutch-drafted final text, which differs only in that the speed originally envisaged has been reduced. Alan Sked discusses these ideas briefly and then puts forward an alternative set of proposals for a united *Europe des patries,* which would allow genuine democratic supervision of the European bureaucracy by a European Parliament, without interfering with the normal processes of national sovereign government. His Parliament would consist of delegates from national parliaments, as opposed to the present set of members directly elected in parallel. The European civil service would cease to have powers of initiation and would be entirely directed by the Council of Ministers, to consist of one specially-appointed Minister for Europe from each national cabinet. The European Court would act as a Supreme Court on the American model, with the sole duty of safeguarding the constitutional treaties and not, as now, the power to extend law in a way designed to enhance the Commission's and its own powers. These ideas are an important attempt to respond to the challenge of designing institutions that would allow Europe to develop its co-operative future without going down the centralist blind alley. They are positive and constructive, giving the lie to critics of the anti-federalists who portray them as unsympathetic to European development.

The book proceeds in Part II to consider first the original *raison d'être* of the EEC: its trade policies, in agriculture and manufactures. Richard Howarth examines the cost, to taxpayers and consumers, of the Common Agricultural Policy. While some other countries, notably Japan, give their farmers more support, the EEC is alone in using a system of price supports rather than one of direct payments ('deficiency payments', as they were called in the UK pre-EEC). Price supports reduce the overt taxpayer cost, but sharply increase the cost to the citizen: because the consumer pays indirectly through higher prices (effectively indirect taxes) instead of through direct taxes, the effect is to distort consumer choice and so reduce welfare overall.

Economists have always criticised such price supports because of their inefficiency: however supports have appealed to some politicians because of their lack of transparency. This seems in particular to have been the case with the EEC. Certain countries were anxious to ensure the protection of their farmers, and were afraid that overt taxpayer costs could prevent agreement between EEC governments forced to find the revenue. Hence the bargain struck in the Rome Treaty: only the CAP system would satisfy those countries and persuade them to agree to free trade in manufactures within the EEC. As Howarth shows that the cost has now escalated to extraordinary levels (£1000 annually per EEC family). These appear to be beyond even the tolerance of France as support spreads well beyond the original farmers of the Six to those recently joined members of the Twelve. As a result at last the system seems to be coming under pressure for reform. But unfortunately it is only limited and insufficient as yet to meet the requirements of the Uruguay Round, which stalled last December over the EEC's unwillingness to make more than a trivial 30 per cent cut in supports over a ten-year period.

This lack of interest in the world trading system suggests that the EEC is unimpressed by the potential gains from free trade, other than within its own borders. Brian Hindley's chapter on EEC actions in dealing with competition from imports confirm this view of the EEC's attitude. Industries whose market shares are threatened by imports from the Far East have lobbied with ease for protection. The EEC's capitulation to these lobbies suggests that it believes there are greater benefits to be had from sustaining 'EEC champions' than from allowing consumers to choose to buy from the best-value source and redeploying resources to where they are more productive – these being the gains from free trade. Yet the 'infant industry' – or in this case 'senile industry' – argument has been, as Brian Hindley notes, decisively rejected by theory and evidence.

He details the method by which the EEC obtains its protectionist ends: 'anti-dumping'. The EEC uses a series of arithmetical devices to ensure that the imports involved are found to be 'dumped'. The process is perceived to be so predetermined that the foreign firms involved usually rush to settle before the decision is reached; settlement usually takes the form of a unilateral rise in import prices. This is bad for the European consumer, creates excess profits for the foreign firm, and damages competition within the EEC. If the anti-dumping action goes ahead, then a duty will be levied, which has the same ill effects apart from the creation of excess profits. Hindley points out that these actions are strictly in contravention of the General Agreement on Tariffs and Trade (GATT), and that a new code is needed to define the arithmetical steps permissible in establishing dumping. At present this is a major loophole in GATT. The truth is that free international competition requires firms to follow pricing strategies in new markets. Sometimes these stress high quality, sometimes low prices: such have been the tools of market penetration throughout the ages. If a World Monopolies Commission were to be asked whether such practices were in restraint of trade – the basic reasoning behind the dumping argument – because prices would later be raised *above* the costs of the home competitors, it would generally answer in the negative and reject the dumping argument. It seems that some such court of appeal in the GATT is needed in the light of the EEC's high-handed use of the anti-dumping loophole. Meanwhile the EEC record in matters of trade inspires little confidence that in the future it would behave in a free trade manner. 'Fortress Europe' looks all too real a possibility, if one is to judge by the past.

Closely related to this protectionist tendency is the EEC's relationship with Eastern Europe, examined by Martin Holmes. The problem is that while EEC countries protest loudly their intention to help their eastern neighbours, they have so far shown no willingness to do so in the most effective way of all – the opening-up of their markets to Eastern European products. Ultimately this opening-up would lead to entry into the EEC for Eastern Europe; again the signs so far are highly ambiguous. 'Widening' has, it has been suggested by highly-placed EEC sources, to wait for 'deepening'. Yet, as Martin Holmes points out, if the EEC markets remain closed to the East, the resulting chaos and underdevelopment could threaten an unstoppable wave of migration westwards, which would be far less welcome to the EEC than extra foreign competition. If only the EEC view of such competition could become warmer, then the obvious benefits to both Eastern and Western Europe of widening could be exploited.

In Part III the authors examine the programme for economic unification. Alan Walters discusses the recent impact of the Exchange Rate Mechanism, I examine the Single Currency, Ben Roberts follows with a discussion of the Social Charter, and Tim Congdon concludes with an examination of tax policies. The 'Walters Critique' of the ERM has been widely accepted. It points out that under the ERM exchange rates can be, and are, fixed in the short term, which implies that higher interest rates can be exploited by foreign exchange traders and investors with limited risk of exchange loss. So short-term nominal interest rates are brought closer together. Yet this produces inappropriate interest rates from a domestic viewpoint: inflationary countries now tend to have low real interest rates (i.e. adjusted for inflation) – the case of Spain for example – and deflationary countries have too high ones – the UK case. The former feed inflation, the latter reinforce deflation. This source of instability can be further exacerbated if fears of a parity change build up: so, for example, in the UK devaluation risk has kept real interest rates higher still.

In his contribution Walters discusses in detail the UK's experience with the ERM, which has been highly deflationary. At one point it seemed possible it could go to the other, Spanish end of the spectrum. However, by entering at an overvalued exchange rate, the deflationary forces in the UK were sharply reinforced while devaluation fears occurred almost immediately. The result has been a severe and stubborn recession. Nor have other countries been free of problems in this turbulent period: Germany has been hampered in its post-unification monetary policies, while other ERM countries are unable to avoid the recessionary effects of its necessary monetary tightening. The ERM is currently being tested more rigorously than in the relatively trouble-free and expansionary 1980s.

In my chapter on EMU, I describe the pressures that have pushed the EEC participants in the ERM into rigid parities. 'Half-baked' as the

ERM is, in the words of Alan Walters, having both fixed and yet adjustable exchange rates, its only hope is to move either to the flexibility of floating or to full fixity. In between, it is bound to be racked by terrible instability which spills over on to economic activity generally. Given the political imperative of moving towards union, a return to floating was not attractive, even though our work shows that it offers the best outcome for Europe as a whole, if combined with intelligent monetary co-ordination.

Hence the EEC has moved towards fixity. By now it is understood that parity changes will occur rarely, if ever. This is close to monetary union *de facto* but without the benefit that the exchange rates set are perceived as irrevocably fixed. As long as there is a risk of parity changes (a 'lack of credibility', in the well-worn phrase), there will be risk premia in wage settlements and interest rates, preventing convergence and damaging traded goods' competitiveness.

Given the drive to fixity, monetary union therefore looks like an objective to be reached as rapidly as possible. However, monetary union has its own problems: countries of very different structures (without convergence in terms of 'real' activity) require flexible exchange rates and interest rates in order to adjust efficiently to differential shocks. Our work shows that instability resulting from such shocks is approximately doubled with monetary union as compared with floating and monetary co-ordination, the regime that remains in Europe's best interests. While it is sometimes said that certain governments are unable to control inflation except through fixing to a stable currency such as the Deutschemark, the truth is that any people desiring stable prices can achieve them more efficiently by exercising domestic monetary control and floating; if so, it is difficult to see why their governments would not please them more by doing this, rather than taking an inefficient alternative.

The Social Charter has been flourished by the socialist politicians of Europe, such as Mrs Papandreou, the Greek Commissioner for Social Affairs, as a key aim of the new Treaty, hinted at but not spelt out in the Single Act. Ben Roberts explains that in fact the Single Act only permits qualified majority voting for measures about health and safety at work; otherwise, unanimity must prevail. Nevertheless the EEC Commission continues to attempt to introduce wide measures, such as the recent proposals for a 48-hour week and no Sunday working, on the narrow grounds of health and safety! Roberts runs through the extensive list of ambitious and interventionist proposals envisaged in the Social Charter: from minimum wages, through entrenched trade union rights, all the way to the Vredeling proposal for worker members of company boards. This is less a social charter than a socialist agenda. It would severely damage the competitiveness of countries with relatively low labour costs, such as Portugal, Spain, Greece and even the UK; this, however, seems partly to be its intention, since entry of low-cost imports from these countries into high-cost countries such as Benelux, France and Germany is referred to as 'social dumping' by some protagonists of this charter.

In an Appendix to Ben Roberts' chapter, Paul Ashton and I estimate the consequences for the UK of the minimum wage proposals that appear to be envisaged in the Social Charter. We find, for example, that the effect on unemployment would be to raise it by 1.5 million (some 6 per cent) if the minimum is set at two-thirds of the UK average wage. Of course, if it was set in relation to the substantially higher EEC average, the consequences would be far worse again. We can only speculate on the effects in other low-cost countries of the EEC – they would undoubtedly be worse than those for the UK, since the gap to be closed by the Charter between their costs and the EC average is so much greater.

We see in the Social Charter a reactionary bid to pull the UK away from its chosen free-market course in social and economic affairs. No wonder Jacques Delors' initiatives have found such a warm welcome on the left of British politics; here is a chance for the left to get its way, though repeatedly defeated at the ballot box. If one takes the social programme of Delors, and adds to it the central budget necessary to support monetary union (coyly referred to in Brussels as 'social and economic cohesion') and the interventionist policies for industry that go with the anti-dumping philosophy discussed above, the cost involved quickly begins to add up to real money. Yet through the 1980s programme of privatisation and spending curbs, the UK has managed to get the share of its GDP devoted to public spending down below 40 per cent, as against shares of nearer 50 per cent through the rest of the EEC.

Tim Congdon discusses the full extent of the current and prospective gap between UK and continental performance in this respect. He notes that if the UK is forced to converge on average EEC behaviour, its tax rates will have to rise sharply, even without allowing for the effects of Delors' implicit spending programme. The one bulwark against such a damaging convergence is competition of tax regimes: naturally, low-tax countries will be relatively attractive to business and so should grow at the expense of others, forcing them to cut taxes for reasons of competitiveness. Given the rest of its programmes, it is no surprise to find that the EEC would like to harmonise tax rates and systems instead. Plainly, to achieve a socialist environment in the EEC, rogue countries offering a more attractive capitalist mixture must be pulled into line. Once again it is a case of Britons, beware!

The pre-Maastricht draft proposals

There is, as the discussion above reveals, a sharp contradiction between widening and deepening Europe. The recently-signed European Economic Area agreement between the EEC and EFTA is a potential step towards the wider Europe that would soon let in Eastern Europe and the ex-Soviet republics. Free trade and free movement of capital would be the key features of this greater Europe. It would be accompanied by political co-operation in keeping the peace, with NATO and the United States retaining their central roles. This Europe would allow free rein to differences of costs, laws, taxes, social security and culture. These would be part of the incentive to exchange goods and move capital. The movement of labour – a serious potential flashpoint – would then be less necessary, notably from Eastern Europe, since poorer areas can grow by trade and investment.

When one reviews the whole of M. Delors' programme, as we have in this book, one is struck by the enormity of the undertaking and its conflict with the drive of recent economic history towards decentralisation and market forces. M. Delors and his allies are determinedly exerting reverse thrust back to the social corporatism experimented with so widely in Europe since the Second World War, with poor if not disastrous consequences, not least in the UK. It is no accident, for example, that Sweden, for so long held up as a model of such an approach, has now turned its back forcefully on it, in the light of increasingly obvious economic strains.

The Maastricht conference proposals can be seen as the latest tactical move in the Delors programme. (Though Delors himself wanted still stronger political proposals, along the lines of the generally rejected Dutch draft for political union, he was realistic enough to retreat.) The proposals were intended to give the EEC Commission and its allies the power to push the programme through, whatever the reluctance of people like the British. However, they had to be agreed unanimously.

Though it is not pleasant to be the odd man out, sometimes saying 'No' is the most positive thing to do. As Maastricht loomed, Britain's veto on these proposals would have greatly strengthened the prospects for an outward-looking Europe.

We now take a look at a representative set of Maastricht proposals, consisting of the Luxembourg draft, together with the Dutch substitute draft for monetary union. These two drafts were in effect amalgamated and tidied up as the basis for discussion at the Maastricht Summit. The Luxembourg draft on political union called for qualified majority voting in the Council of Ministers on a vast range of subjects. They included social security, transport, EC 'general economic policy', economic 'advice' to member states, the Social Charter, training, R&D subsidies, energy and environmental interventions, industrial policy, tourism, and consumer protection.

The main EC authority would have remained the Council, but the European Parliament would also have obtained authority to pass EC laws, with supranational authority. Up to now the Council has merely agreed directives which then must be implemented by national parliaments to become (national) law. The Luxembourg draft would have changed all that. If the Council decided by qualified majority that a law was needed, it could have submitted one to the Parliament, to adopt, reject (the end of the process) or amend. If it disagreed with Parliament's amendments, a Conciliation Committee was to be convened to obtain agreement between them. Once Parliament and the Council agreed on a proposal, it would have become law.

Article W stipulated a conference in 1996 to amend the Treaty further 'in the perspective of strengthening the federal character of the Union'; and it permitted others to be convened at any time on a proposal from any member state. So Maastricht made provision for its own perpetuation, ensuring a permanent spotlight on the European issue, with the 'isolation' of those who are not '*communautaire*' and the accompanying *brouhaha*.

In the areas of defence and foreign policy the draft was modest, calling for qualified majority voting only on the 'implementation' of jointly agreed common policies. The Dutch draft went further and created a furore which led to its withdrawal – but this may have given the Luxembourg draft a false respectability. Even if drastically modified, the Luxembourg draft must in time have committed us to a federal centralised Europe across the whole of economic policy. The creeping process, by which the Commission administers and the European Court backs its administrative extensions in the continental tradition, would then have pushed centralism forward.

The Dutch draft on monetary union allowed any country to opt out of the single currency; a minimum number of countries that have met tough criteria of (monetary) convergence could agree to go ahead after 1997. Much was made in the UK debate of our ability to opt out. But this was of only limited help. Most of the eleven, if not all, would be enabled, if these criteria were weakly applied, to go ahead at full speed as part of an amended Treaty. There would then inevitably be major problems: monetary convergence does not imply convergence in the sense of market integration, which is the proper measure of fitness for a shared currency. To help them cope with differential shocks under the single currency, large-scale tranfers would be needed to less advanced areas such as Spain, Greece, Portugal and the Italian South. To save money, there would then be pressure for alternative policy instruments: industrial intervention, protection, price supports paid for by the consumer – all of them available within the extended Treaty as proposed. We may or may not have eventually joined this single currency, but we would have been committed to participating in these developments. And quite apart from these pressures there would have been the ongoing saga of the Social Charter and the endless lobbying for European industrial subsidy and protection ('anti-dumping'), which would have further emasculated the already weakened competition laws.

This 'deeper' Europe would be hard for the wider Europe to penetrate. It would create two tiers in Europe – the rich but ossified and over-regulated centre, and the generally poorer periphery denied full access to the centre's markets. If some or all of the EFTA group were to join the centre it would not resolve the contradiction. They, like us, would be pulled both ways: to become part of an inward-looking bloc, or to stay out as part of its periphery. If outside the centre, they and we would risk being denied free access for our key products (such as cars from Japanese factories in the UK), on the grounds we had not implemented all the provisions, social and other, of the EC 'playing field'.

If, on the other hand, we were to have said 'No' to any Treaty amendments, standing pat on the existing, largely liberal Treaty with its Single Act, then this inward-looking centre could not have developed. Those who wanted tighter uni- or multi-lateral links could have formed them in 'the room next door', where they would have been prevented by the existing Treaty from retreating into protection. Meanwhile the pressures of the outside world would have pushed the EC, however recalcitrant, into reducing its trade barriers – towards the East on pain of mass migration and chaos, and towards the rest of the western world on pain of general retaliation.

The British worked hard at Maastricht to eliminate some and dilute others of these proposals, though they did not say 'No' overall. I now turn to the resulting Maastricht agreement itself.

The Maastricht agreement

In the event, the Maastricht agreement could have been much worse. It would have been better to have said 'No'. The Tory Maastricht Seven who voted against were right to do so. But once the political judgement was taken not to upset our neighbours in this way, the Major exercise became one of damage limitation. It succeeded up to a point.

On monetary union the UK has its opt-in clause and agreement on tough criteria (apparently to be rigorously applied) for the Single Currency to go ahead. It also succeeded in blocking the infamous unemployment-generating social chapter for Britain: if the others truly want to lumber themselves with it, that will be their privilege. The extension of qualified majority voting within the Council of Ministers and the provision of veto powers for the Euro-Parliament have been rigorously limited: the final Treaty is but a shadow of the Luxembourg (let alone the Dutch) draft in these respects. But there is no room for complacency. The centralising, socialising federal tendency has a foot in the door. Those of us that believe in a free-market, outward-looking Europe cannot relax our efforts. There will be more Maastrichts elsewhere: the next is in 1996, as provided for in the original draft, though with no reference now to federalism (all such references now having being expunged).

Politically, the main hostages to fortune are first, the extension of qualified majority voting, mainly to environment, education and cross-border infrastructure; and secondly, the veto powers of the Euro-Parliament, mainly on Single Market measures. The idea here seems to have been to surrender power only on matters closely related to the Single Market. The problem is that the Commission and the European Court have used every extension 'constructively', to smuggle measures unobtainable under unanimity through these looser channels. Nor do we yet know how the Parliament will behave with its veto, which is a powerful bargaining instrument. The chances are that all three institutions will be pushing the same way – towards corporatism and protectionism.

We shall just have to wait and see. Ultimately politics will rule, and if the overall arrangements do not suit us we will have to change them. As Britain represents a fifth of the EC's GNP and population, 'eleven to one' is an empty threat to us, as the discussion of the social chapter showed. An EC without Britain is as credible as a Russian Commonwealth without the Ukraine. In fact, the EC and that Commonwealth may well turn out have a lot in common, materially as well as constitutionally, as time goes on. The 1990s will see the building of the European Space, and we will have many allies in that process for an open Europe.

On the economic side, matters look more promising from our viewpoint, though again the risks are there. The much-trumpeted monetary union will be delayed until 1999, as there will not be enough countries (seven are needed) to satisfy the criteria by 1997. Even in 1999, only those who satisfy them can go ahead: that may well only be four or five. The Netherlands, Luxembourg and France may well persuade the Bundesbank to let them have some extra seats on its board, for that is what the Euro-Bank will amount to. Belgium, Ireland and Italy will be keen but too debt-ridden; and the southern countries would be too expensive. This outcome may well be less and later than would have occurred outside a new treaty.

This is a summary judgement. Let us go into more detail. The criteria for 'convergence', to be met by each country entering the Single Currency, are that: its inflation rate should in the previous year be no more than 1.5 per cent (and its long-term interest rates no more than 2 per cent) above that of the three best performers in the group; its budget deficit should not (normally) be more than 3 per cent, and its public debt 60 per cent, of Gross Domestic Product; and its currency should have remained in the narrow band for two years without a devaluation. At present only three countries fulfil these criteria: France, Luxembourg and Denmark. Belgium's debt is over 100 per cent of GDP, as is Italy's and Ireland's; even The Netherlands' is 78 per cent. Germany's deficit is 5 per cent of GDP; Greece's 17 per cent. Spain's inflation is 7 per cent, Portugal's 15 per cent. And so on.

So one view, which appeared to be that of Norman Lamont in the BBC's 'On the Record' pre-Maastricht, and that of the government off the record since, is that monetary union is not likely to go ahead in the foreseeable future. That seemed a dangerous assumption in the heady days of 1991 when European integration seemed to be on a floodtide, with economic worries tossed to one side. Rules and criteria can be changed, and in the last resort statistics massaged and 'normally' stretched. The fate of the Madrid Conditions for our joining of the Exchange Rate Mechanism is instructive: we were told they were 'fulfilled prospectively'!

However, 1992, the strains of recession and the tough line on interest rates being taken by the Bundesbank have changed all that. German public opinion has woken up to the dangers of losing the beloved Deutschemark: Kohl is felt to have given too much away. The harsh criteria for joining the Single Currency will be insisted upon as long as this mood lasts. It is likely to last. The Bundesbank is profiting from it to re-establish its leadership in monetary affairs, so prejudiced by Kohl over reunification and now over Maastricht, about which the Bundesbank was far from enthused. The Bank gets its power, not from the constitution, but from popular sentiment about inflation. Inflation is running at 4.5 per cent and not yet falling: the German people are in no mood for sentimentality about European unity with such dangers around.

Behind the explicit criteria for monetary union also lie much deeper problems, which are not merely monetary and financial. What is truly needed for monetary union is the substantial integration of the economies involved, like that between Wales and England. This means either that their industries are so intertwined that a shock in one region is a similar shock in another, so that there is little need for exchange rates (or relative prices) of the two regions to move. Or else labour must move so easily between them that again there is no need for prices to move. Neither of these is remotely true of any group of EEC countries, with the possible exception of the Benelux countries and Germany.

Once such integration occurs, then also the nuisance value (to business and tourists) of having to change currencies across the borders becomes a significant cost (as opposed to the trivial size identified by the EEC Commission within Europe at present). Before it occurs there will on balance be the substantial economic costs of a Single Currency, not just the political costs of losing sovereignty. Businessmen are quite naturally aware of the direct savings to their own businesses of not having to hedge foreign exchange risk or exchange currency denominations within Europe. However, these benefits of a Single Currency are quite simply overwhelmed by the wider costs – of higher and more unstable output and employment – which occur indirectly through the lack of integration (see the chapter on monetary union below).

These costs are, as today's potentially much milder experience with the Exchange Rate Mechanism illustrates, of extreme consequence to business, not to speak of the people of Britain generally. And the costs apply equally to other European countries, as they too will realise in the grim recession that lies ahead for them. The late 1990s will not be propitious for monetary union. Like the earlier 1970s proposals for monetary union by 1980, those of Maastricht will probably be postponed *sine die* and will at best only involve a tiny DM area.

Conclusions

The aim of this book is to inform debate and to inject greater caution into public commentary on the projects for European unification emerging from Brussels and some other continental sources. The facts, we submit, and solid academic analysis suggest that many of these projects have been ill-thought-out and either have already harmed or would in the future seriously damage the people of Europe. It would indeed be sad if Project Europe turns out to have a large cost, and to enjoy benefits that are at best few, and at worst mere political sops to vested interests. Such a construction would not stand the test of time; it would eventually create tensions that could destroy it. If by good fortune those tensions instead spawned a better structure, then at the very least we would have lost much from all the waste and conflict of such a false start. The inconclusive muddle of the final Maastricht compromise agreement gives all of us in Europe a few years to clear our minds and formulate a viable structure. We hope that when the future of Europe is again discussed in the Maastricht-equivalent in 1996, ideas will be better formed and a better route forward will be chosen.

PART I

WHAT SORT OF POLITICAL UNION?

2 *Norman Stone*

History casts doubts on the Euro-dream

The radiant dawn begins with a fine drizzle – or, rather, a rain of petty directives about the content of prawn crackers. 'Europe' is a jolly good idea. It is the realisation of quite an old dream – that of Gladstone or Mazzini, in which liberally-run countries co-operate in peace and prosperity, acting as a model for less fortunate peoples in the world outside. The single market – free trade all round – has already done its bit for everyone's welfare. The prospect of a united Western Europe has been, I believe, one of the most important factors in the collapse of communism. Eastern Europeans and Russians looked at 'Europe' and realised the communist game was up.

These are the grand headlines of 'Europe' and there is much in them. The trouble is that grand headlines have a way of dissolving into miles of small print. That is what happened in the run-up to Maastricht. Like testudos in a Roman siege, embattled armies of committees with wads of paper were having to sort out 'unity' under twenty five different headings. There was to be a European policy on the environment, on education, on culture, on social affairs, on tourism, on this, on that. The bureaucratic prose went on and on, to the point at which it became impossible to sort out the leaves from the twigs, let alone the trees from the wood. It left the vast majority of 'Europeans' absolutely cold. In this country only about a third of us bother to vote in Euro-elections, and fewer still can name their Euro-MP. In other countries the situation is not much better, though on the Continent to be European is to be respectable particularly in Germany, where they are frightened of their own past.

In all this mass of documentation, two things stood out. The first was that the Commission in Brussels really does want to see a Europe with a Single Currency, run by an updated version of Napoleonic prefects –

the sort of people who know best what is good for the rest of us, and do not want to be bothered with tiresome and irresponsible democratic organisations. Various continental Europeans are quite inclined towards this idea. The smaller countries – the Dutch, the Portuguese – like the notion because it makes them feel important. Again, in some other countries people mistrust their own government. Italy is the best case. Italian government is a notorious mess and already one-third of the electorate in the North is set to vote for the *Lega Lombarda*, which wants to break free of Italy and, in effect, join up with southern Germany. To them, Europe is the saviour, laying down rules which will prevent excessive taxation, corruption, and the Mafia. Throw into this the 'geopolitical' question of Germany, and you complete the picture. A big Germany with 80 million people is supposed to be tied into a new Europe in order that the old German Adam can be controlled. So we had economic and political union for discussion at Maastricht with a lot of support.

The second consideration was that British interests are not necessarily involved with this. We do not mistrust our governments in the same way. In many ways a united Europe would work to our disadvantage. For instance, over matters of immigration we do not need, as an island, to have the same policy as countries with an open land frontier. In education, unity would clearly make us a thumping loss.

In theory, all Europeans will be able to attend each other's universities at the same cost as the natives. All Continentals who want to learn English, the universal language, will rush to us. Yet the fees at British universities are set at a level which the natives' government feels it can afford – in the case of Oxford, rather absurdly, about two-thirds of what you pay for an 8-year-old to go to a private school. In other words, come 'unification' in Europe, the British taxpayer could be subsidising the better-off Continentals' children to learn English.

I mention these lesser matters of unity only to show that, for us, the question of Europe is not at all a simple matter of international benevolence. When you get into the larger questions, the doubts continue. For instance, I do not believe in handing power to the Euro-Parliament because I know no historical precedent at all for an international parliament ever working. The European Parliament, with, at Maastricht, some German support, wants more power. Many of its members are anxious to do good, and, to be fair to them, they have already done so – taking, for instance, an interest in human rights. Archduke Otto (the historian in me cannot be brought to write 'Dr von Habsburg') has championed the Croats and Slovenes, and done much for their morale by publicising their cause at Strasbourg: all honour to him. But I am afraid that the example of the old Habsburg Parliament in Vienna is a savage deterrent for advocates of multi-nationalist bodies. The nationality groups fought each other over endless trivialities, of shattering tediousness, such as the language you put first on postage stamps, and in the end *everything* boiled down to nonsense. Budgets had to be passed by decree, and in 1914 they closed it down. Belgium today seems to be heading in this direction, as Walloons slug it out with Flemings; efforts to force Serbs and Croats to work together in Yugoslavia have broken down dramatically. So the case for a functioning Euro-Parliament is not historically at all strong. The 'democratic deficit' in that sense can only be wildly applauded – for, again historically, the only way to run multinational outfits is by bureaucratic absolutism.

Now, we should be fair about this. It *is* certainly true that 'Brussels' is not overmanned – the whole of 'Europe' *does* count fewer people than, say, our Scottish Office. We should also admit that the tradition of snooty prefects *has* worked quite well in, say, Paris transport issues or German regional policy. A well-trained local government with real powers is important – and northern English cities have suffered vastly for lack of one (compare Liverpool and, say Bremen, which had similar problems). But the snooty prefects can get out of control – and though their own numbers at present are not high, could grow uncontrollably, with hideous architecture to match. They have already in one sense started to subvert the proposals of the Single Act of 1986. When we all signed up, it was upon the understanding that, according to the famous *Cassis de Dijon* court case of France *vs*. Germany, one country's goods should go into another country without being blocked by reason of (alleged or real) hygienic deficiencies: in the Community, said the Court, the standards of each country should be accepted elsewhere. That way, there was no barrier to free trade. The Single Act followed. Yet Brussels has interpreted it to interfere in every nook and cranny – Morecambe Bay prawns have to be boiled in clean sea-water; Italian contraceptives must be a millimetre longer, and so forth. There was no need for this, yet any student of public choice will not be surprised at it. And though Brussels does not contain too many people now, think of the armies of people in each country, busied with making people conform to 'European standards'. Force nations to co-operate, and you end in farce. Let them work together informally and you sometimes do quite well.

The clincher here is the European currency. Artificial currencies, and central banks uncontrolled by democratic assemblies, while enjoying a good reputation today, did not, in the early 1930s, have a good reputation at all. Instead, they made the great slump worse than it needed to be (and as a result the Bank of England was nationalised after the war, specifically to prevent a repetition). Why impose a straitjacket if it is not the outcome of an evolution we have yet to see?

For these reasons there is some cause for scepticism about Britain-in-Europe. The fact is that other countries – the French and Germans, in particular – have some of the same doubts. The German association of entrepreneurs, ASU, came out in November 1991, for instance, with a *Memorandum on European Integration*, arguing for 'competition between systems, with the furthest possible reduction or setting-aside of central powers of direction'. It must be 'open for extension, especially to the East', and internally it must take account of the political, cultural and economic pluralism which makes for Europe's identity'. The same organisation – it represents that middle section of German industry that has been such a powerful force since the 1950s – expresses strong doubt as to the removal of the Bundesbank's unique role, and is even sceptical as to the proposed regional policies of Maastricht. Money transfers from rich to poor regions have worked in Germany; but the poor regions there were in fact relatively rich, and regional policy tends to be the more successful where it is less necessary. I doubt if there is now a single North Italian to be found who would argue that shovelling northern money into the South would do anything other than enrich the Mafia. Many people on the Continent share these doubts. Their spokesmen cannot say so openly – Germans because they are scared of the Germans, the French because they are scared of the Germans. We have the lead hand in opposing unreality and silliness in European matters, and are closer to the truth than many official Europeans.

It would greatly strengthen the government's ongoing stand against the Euro-silliness if it were to hold out the possibility of a referendum on the Maastricht agreement. After all, we have been asked, even in the final agreement, to give up our currency and parts of a long tradition of parliamentary government and of the rule of law, and to accept much that has made the continental states what they are. The groundswell of opinion here is building up against the kind of dead Europe being proposed. A referendum would educate and clarify popular opinion on these issues and signal to other European countries what British opinion will and will not stomach. Yes, referendums have to be used with care. But on a matter such as this, why not? We have done it before and we should do it again. The people, curiously enough, often get things right. The British voted *for* Europe nearly twenty years ago. But it was not for *this* Europe; and the fear must now be that, in answer to fiscal and monetary straitjackets, and to the economic sclerosis which they portend, the enlightened absolutists of Brussels will provoke the peasant revolts that their counterparts always did provoke in European history. What price a Euro-Poujade ?

3 *Alan Walters*

The Brussels Leviathan

Some years ago M. Jacques Delors said that 80 per cent of the economic and social legislation applicable in the United Kingdom would eventually come from Brussels. At the time many, myself included, thought that these were simply the extravagant aspirations of that distinguished Eurocrat. Quite beyond the pale. But the intervening years have taught me, and perhaps others, an important lesson: never underestimate the ingenuity and sheer ability and drive of the high-level bureaucrats of the Community. They know what they want – a highly centralised United States of Europe – and they pursue it with the tenacity of Talleyrand and the drive of de Gaulle. Yet I suspect that most people in the European Community do not want a central all-powerful federal government in Brussels controlling some 80 per cent of their legislation. Certainly British opinion, except among a small minority of Euro-enthusiasts, is quite opposed to any such domination by a federal government.

The general idea of forming a United States of Europe to counterbalance the United States of America has, however, haunted many a European breast. To transform a gaggle of bickering second rate powers into one superpower, which may even put the United States in the shade, would be a massive reassertion of Europe's political supremacy after its eclipse half a century ago. The economic strength is already there; all that is needed is the political leadership. The absence of a popular consensus does not deter the federalist faction. But the federalists have a dilemma. It is difficult to find any successful examples of federation among culturally disparate peoples such as those of the existing Community. The shining exception appears to be the United States. But the United States was not a union of different states or peoples that retained their own languages, legal systems, *kulturs*, etc. It was a melting-pot with the English language and law recognised as the dominant common ingredient. Even so, it took America's most bloody war to settle the issue of the rights of secession and slavery.

Elsewhere federation has fared badly. Nowadays we seem to be surrounded by disintegrating unions. The Soviet Union has been held together by successive tyrannies and is now falling apart. Yugoslavia as a political unit has largely gone. But what of the democratic federations, of peoples of disparate language, law and culture ? Perhaps the only example is that of Canada, by no means a melting-pot, where the separate language and customs of French Quebec are enshrined in the constitution. (The native Canadians have also some protection, but for simplicity I ignore them.) The immense cost of bilingualism, the massive transfers of money, the politics of exploitation have caused grave doubts about whether the Canadian state will hold together, however costly dismemberment might be.

Europe is no Canada. It has more than twelve languages, and very different customs and mores. And with their long history, the nation-states of Europe have even more reason to guard their language, customs, queens and culture. The cultural divides of Canada are minor compared with those in Europe – so much so that to call for a federal republic seems quite absurd and to risk a fate far worse than that of Canada. Perhaps that is why even such enthusiasts as M. Delors do not openly advocate a federal republic of Europe. And their ilk in Britain, such as Michael Heseltine and Sir Geoffrey Howe, also are adamant that Europe should be no more than a confederation of sovereign states, at least for now.

But those who would wish to see a federal Europe can pursue their aim more deviously and, at least in political terms, more astutely, by promoting the cause of closer integration of monetary policies in Europe. This integration is seen to be the wholesale participation in the Exchange Rate Mechanism (ERM), so that every country is in the mechanism with the narrow bands, with realignments only to be agreed *in extremis*. (This is the Heseltine-Howe position or stage II of Delors.) I have set out in some detail in my book *Sterling in Danger* the enormous strains of holding the stage II Delors system together. Such fatal flaws have also been recognised by Karl Otto Pohl as well as the economists on the Delors committee. Stage II of Delors is simply not viable. One way out would be to go back to floating the currencies. But the political situation will not admit what many in Europe would regard as a major climb-down and defeat. The pressure is on for full monetary union – with absolutely fixed exchange rates, and then one currency to rule us all.

But in order to have one fiat currency for Europe, there must needs be a high degree of political union. The case for one money is the case for a federal republic, but it is much easier to get a constituency for one money than for federal rule. A centralised federal Europe will follow, as night follows day. The need for a political union to support a monetary union can be easily observed in all federal states. First, with the differential impact of a single monetary policy, for example on the poor South, very large subsidies will be needed to hold the union together (as in Canada). The federal government will need to have access to large amounts of tax revenue, and so it will require a strong central political authority to levy those taxes and supervise the subsidies. The wrangling that took place in the present political structure of the EEC for relatively quite small subsidies points up the inadequacy of the present structure for the great transfers required by monetary union.

Secondly the concentration of power in the political arm of the Community to carry through 'international monetary policy', including the fixing of exchange rates of the ECU against the dollar and yen, is one of the axioms of the draft structure of the Central Bank of Europe. This monetary foreign policy is a natural concomitant of political foreign policy. Europe will need to react quickly, to speak with one voice, in order to deal with the USA, Japan, the NICs and so on. The extension to one defence policy subsumes the vital national interests completely in Brussels. Thirdly, the immense power of a Central Bank of Europe will have to be counterbalanced by a central political authority of equal or greater weight.

To counter this argument, one may protest that one can surely set up a monetary union with fixed exchange rates and still retain political independence. The obvious example is the old gold standard system which ruled throughout the West, with the occasional hiatus, from the 1870s through to 1931. But the gold standard was a commodity currency. Under the old gold standard the quantity of money was outside the hands of any authority; it was determined by the technology and idiosyncracies of gold production. As the old gold standard eroded and as the fiat dollar became the basis for the system, power over monetary policy shifted to the monetary authorities – primarily the United States. It was the disparate interests of the United States and the Europeans which saw the collapse of the pegged exchange rate dollar-based system of Bretton Woods. The floating rate system was the only one consistent with national governments, with their different agendas and objectives.

The ECU, which is to be the currency of monetary union, is certainly not planned as a commodity currency. There is to be no abnegation of power on the part of Brussels to an automatic standard. The ECU will be a fiat currency with no commodity, gold or real peg. Its behaviour will be in the hands of the eighteen member board of the Central Bank of Europe. National aspirations will have to conform to their uniform policies, and that conformation can only be achieved through a strong federal authority.

If I am correct in this argument, one would surely conclude that it is much better to discuss and debate the real issue – a federal *vs.* a confederate Europe. Then the covert political issues would be overt and on the table. Let us see where the people of Europe stand on these fundamental forms of European union. This is anathema to the federalists, for they rightly fear that common opinion is not on their side. But the Delors bandwagon rolls on with all its technical achievements and few to question where it is going. British Europhiles are anxious to get in the driving seat, but alas it has only one fixed track and one destination.

Unfortunately I believe that Britain has already taken the first steps down the slippery slope towards a monetary union. Whatever protests may be put forward that the ERM does not necessarily imply a monetary union and concomitant political union, it will be very difficult for Britain to reverse up the slippery slope. So much political capital has been invested on this path to a union.

During the autumn of 1991, we have seen Mr. Major's performance on the high wire, tilting further and further to monetary union, while protesting that no Britain will never enter a union without a yea vote from parliament. Ostensibly designed to placate those in the party that fear federalism, the assurance is a really a cynical political trick. Tied firmly to the mark or ECU by the apron strings as we would be for some six years, by 1997 the cost of any withdrawal will seem overwhelming compared with the comfortable policy of cocooning Britain in the monetary union. The anti-federalists will be marginalised as diehards or even dinosaurs, fossils of a past and troubled age.

I had always believed that a monetary union of Europe was virtually impossible because the people would strongly oppose the political union that was required. I did not foresee the astuteness of those like M. Delors who represent each of the steps as perfectly consistent with quite reasonable reductions in national power and sovereignty. It was all very *communautaire*. Perhaps that is why the venom of the Europhiliacs turned on Mrs Thatcher, who insisted on putting the full agenda on the table. Alas, formidable though she is, even the Iron Lady was no match for the Delors bandwagon.

As I look back on my analysis of the monetary and political union of Europe, I cannot help noting the increasing pessimism. It is tempting to look back and ask: where did we go wrong? I supported, but with no great enthusiasm, Britain's entry into Europe in 1971 – mainly because I thought free European trade would protect the people of Britain against the depredations of socialist governments. How wrong I was! Yet in those days the de Gaulle concept was of *Europe des patries*; there was no thought of monetary or political union. (Indeed, I recollect Mr Heath making specific denials of that kind.) Even the Single European Act of 1985 made no mention, except in a parenthetical remark about 'coordination', of monetary union – although it certainly should have alerted us all with its talk of 'an ever closer union'.

In my view, however, the crucial surrender of Britain came in 1987, when Nigel Lawson pegged sterling to the Deutschemark. That was the politically irreversible step into the ERM, so into EMU, and so into a centralised and increasingly socialist United States of Europe. The federalists have enjoyed one Eurotic victory after another for the last four years. The Danes may have delayed, but I fear, not stopped the federalists.

Many people (for example David Owen) continue to believe that through some constitutional constraints – such as insistence on unanimity for all critical decisions – the centralised power can be contained and tamed. Others (such as Genscher) seek to expand the powers of the Strasbourg parliament to introduce democratic accountability to the Euro-Leviathan. I would not rely on such devices or parliaments. Rules of unanimity (such as in Poland's Sejm) have completely hobbled what must be a very active and intervening government, and the pressure for a 'working' system such as majority rule, however qualified, will be irresistible. And whether more democratic oversight is introduced seems to me to be a minor matter.

The real problem is the *concentration* of power, democratic or not. Indeed, the institution of democratic approval may induce a greater surrender of powers to the Brussels behemoth. And we have many sad examples of democratic tyrannies (M. Delors may reflect on the popular support in his own country for the terror of the 1790s).

It is tragically easy to destroy great institutions. It is dauntingly difficult to build a society with the tolerance, diversity and responsiveness which are characteristic of the present United Kingdom. Mrs Thatcher realised this – and she lost her political life in unflinchingly defending our freedoms. Now it is Mr Major's turn. We can only hope that he will not give away the shop.

4 *Alan Sked*

A proposal for European union

After many years of subterfuge and dissimulation, Europe's federalists have come out of their closet. They are now openly demanding a 'European superstate'[1] and claiming that a second superpower is necessary to maintain a world balance of power against the United States. In the words of Horst Teltschik, until very recently head of the foreign affairs section of the West German Federal Chancellery:[2]

It is a good thing for every superpower to have a rival of equal strength, keeping the scales in balance. The history of the last few decades shows there are many states on this planet which favour having a counterweight to the USA or an alternative : as a European, I say that a Europe in the process of integration should take on such a role.

At the same time European federalists hold that such a superpower could be lightly governed through a federal system. Their model is the German one, with the German government, banking and electoral systems poised to take over Europe. Germany works, they say, so why should not a German-based Europe?

Much as one admires the post-war West German record, one has to look at the *revers de la medaille*, that is to say, the right claimed by Brussels to interfere in everything. 'Subsidiarity' – last year's buzzword – is clearly now a thing of the past; the Commission's official opinion on the Luxembourg draft treaty contains blanket clauses which would make it nothing less than an Enabling Act. For example, its proposed amendment to clause 3(c) reads: 'The union shall have the resources needed to attain the objectives it has set itself and to carry through the policies to that end.' There is no provision at all for democratic control. And even federalism gives way to the demand for a 'unitary state' ('...consistency can be guaranteed in full only if the construction of the Community is conceived on a unitary basis', Clause 3) with single, foreign, defence, monetary, fiscal, regional, commercial, transport, social, environmental, educational, agricultural, fisheries, regional and cultural policies. On offer, in other words, is a top-heavy, centralised, bureaucratic and unaccountable polity where national governments might as well be headed by the Minister of Sport. Indeed, even he or she would be in danger, as Euro-teams began to emerge. In practice, therefore, the German model is a mirage. A united Europe would be very different – far more centralised, far less accountable, and far more bureaucratic.

There are also other reasons why a united Europe would not be like the West Germany of old. That state worked for a variety of reasons: it had an homogeneous and cohesive population; it had no world role to worry about or pay for; it did not have to borrow money; it had a folk-hatred of inflation; it had a work ethic strengthened by the need for national rehabilitation after the *Hitlerzeit*; it respected the rule of law; and its political class were aware of the need to maintain high standards in public life, even if they often fell short of them. None of these factors will pertain in a united Europe. Our putative federal superstate will resemble Nigeria or India more than Germany or the USA.

For a start it will remain a hodgepodge of nationalities, despite all the efforts to create a European nationalism through devices such as a common flag, a common anthem or a common passport. Europe will lack that common public opinion, therefore, which alone makes government truly accountable. Many of the nations concerned, moreover, will have no strong tradition of democracy. This is already true today. In Italy, for example, large parts of the South are run by the Mafia and are out of government control; as a result, the fastest growing political movements in the North are those which call for separation from the South (including Rome) before the country as a whole is overtaken by corruption. The murder rate is appalling. The political system is commonly held to be bankrupt, and desperate popular efforts are being made to reform it by referendum. In Greece, the economy is almost beyond hope, with the former prime minister on trial. In Spain, the present prime minister did not bother to appear in parliament for seven months; likewise his ministers are under no obligation to turn up even to answer censure debates. Even in France, the parliament (to use the textbook phrase) is 'rationalised' – i.e. it has no control over the executive, while the prospect of mass immigration plus the sense of lost national identity has led to riots all over the country and the possibility of a neo-fascist President.[3]

Germany for its part is witnessing the rise of a new neo-Nazi movement with physical attacks on immigrants, asylum-seekers and 'southern-looking' foreigners. Meanwhile, at the very heart of Europe, the Commission itself is affected by nepotism. Political connections are required to obtain jobs with influence, let alone power. This same Commission estimates that the Community loses at least £6 billion each year through fraud.[4] This distinctly depressing situation is hardly likely to be improved by the accession of East European states, with no recent democratic tradition, which will be suffering from major economic problems and a desperate need for loans, not to mention the accession of Austria, where virulent anti-semitism still exists.[5] There, 30 per cent of the population would object to Jewish neighbours, while over 30 per cent believe that Jews 'exploit' the memory of the Holocaust and would do better to stop complaining about it. In short, if the federalists get their way, a highly centralised, bureaucratic system based on a corrupt political ethos is likely to be the shape of the new (anti-American) European superstate.

For Great Britain, the outlook might be particularly grim. Along with Germany, she would remain the major contributor to a rapidly expanding European budget. (Billions of pounds in transfer costs will be needed to bribe the Southern European states to accept monetary union.) Yet unlike Germany, Britain would receive relatively little in return. Already each British family of four in the land today has to pay a full cost of about £1,000 a year to sustain the CAP (for details see Richard Howarth's chapter, this volume). The mismanagement of fisheries policy means that fish stocks may be so seriously depleted in the North Sea that the fishing fleet will become redundant. If European Political and Monetary Union were to go ahead, Parliament would lose its 'power of the purse' and *raison d'etre*; unemployment would soar; budget deficits would be tightly constricted necessitating rising taxes and reduced welfare programmes during recessions; identity cards and armed police would be introduced following the abolition of national frontiers; while British troops could be sent to fight wars in support of policies dictated by majority vote. Quite in contradiction to conventional beliefs, the City would suffer from Economic and Monetary Union, since increased regulation from Brussels would drive lucrative 'offshore banking' to New York and Japan. Democratic control designed to limit these disasters would be exercised neither in Britain nor in Europe, with the result that there would be riots here as well. These would be part of the nationalist backlash which would sweep Europe soon after the consequences of Political and Monetary Union became known. In short, the newly created supra-national superpower would quickly disintegrate under the weight of its own ambition.

This in fact has been the destiny of almost every multi-national state in history: the old European Empires; the USSR; Yugoslavia; Pakistan, the British post-colonial federations (the Central African, the East African, the West Indian, the Malaysian); Canada is already tottering over the Quebec problem; India is saved by the use of force in Nagaland and Kashmir; Nigeria overcame Biafra only by force; while China retains Tibet in the same way. How long would the USA, one wonders, remain intact if a number of states were to choose Spanish as their official language? (One should not forget that the USA itself only survives thanks to the outcome of its civil war; no state is allowed as a result to secede.) One is tempted to formulate a law of historical development: *all multi-national states break up and the more democracy that is introduced, the sooner they break up.* (The apparent exception which proves the rule is Switzerland, but even there one has to remember that federalism was imposed on the state by the victors of the Swiss Civil War in 1847.)

A Europe united politically and economically in the manner proposed by Delors and others is thus likely to be a Frankenstein's monster. The question which arises is whether an alternative Europe could be built. My belief is that it could, but it would require a great deal of modesty from our present generation of Eurocrats and would entail a complete re-examination of their assumptions. The following four, for example – and they comprise the major pillars of contemporary Eurofederalist thought – would have to be abandoned immediately:

1) that the nation-state is obsolescent;

2) that a United States of Europe would be like the United States of America;

3) that a federally united Europe is needed to defend European interests against America and Japan; and

4) that federalists stand for peace and progress, whereas those who defend national sovereignty are old-fashioned nationalists who live in the past.

On the first claim, the truth is that the most successful states today are nation-states: Japan, the USA and Germany – whereas large multi-national states are almost everywhere in difficulties: the (defunct) USSR, Yugoslavia, India and Nigeria, for example. In Asia, meanwhile, it is the small states which are forging ahead economically – Taiwan, Singapore, Hong Kong and South Korea – without any apparent need to pool their currencies or form a federal union out of ASEAN. In Eastern Europe, likewise, the former satellite states of the Soviet empire appear in no way ready to surrender their new-found national independence. The nation-state is hardly obsolete; nor is bigger better. Indeed, recent research into the question of why Europe, rather than India, China or Arabia surged ahead economically and technologically after the fourteenth century points to the fact that Europe remained divided, whereas the Mogul, Ming and Ottoman Empires, by militarily and bureaucratically uniting these other parts of the world, helped destroy their ability to adapt. Europe's historic success, in other words, has been due to her diversity rather than her political or administrative unity.

The second claim that there is an analogy between a United States of Europe and the United States of America is quite clearly misleading. It fails to recognise that the American colonists were a fairly homogeneous group who were starting government from scratch. Europe today is definitely not starting from scratch; rather, it contains nations whose histories go back almost a thousand years. They are culturally diverse and speak a large number of different languages. Finally, they have developed different political institutions, many of which would find themselves in direct competition with any European federal government. A true analogy between Europe and America, therefore, would only arise were the USA to form a United States of the Americas with Brazil, Ecuador, Mexico, Argentina, Peru, Chile, etc., with a federal capital in, say, Managua, and with a common currency managed by a system of largely Latin American banks. This is not a prospect which appeals to the many supporters of European unity who are to be found today in the United States.

The third claim that Europe requires a federal government to protect its interests against Japan and the United States is based upon incorrect assumptions, as is another argument that only a European federal government can prevent war breaking out between France and Germany. It must surely be true that Europe today is already sufficiently united to fulfil both these tasks. There is no danger any longer of a Franco-German war, while the European Commission has proved perfectly capable, in all sorts of commercial negotiations, of protecting European trading interests around the world.

With respect to the fourth claim, the persistence of such arguments highlights the way in which it is the European federalists who still think in old-fashioned terms about the international system and the world balance of power. Far from being progressive anti-nationalists, seeking to put an end to the inherently dangerous competition between nation-states, their real objective is to construct a larger nation-state called 'Europe', which, with its own national sovereignty, will prove able to indulge in that competition more efficiently on a global scale. By talking of a 'European culture' and 'European interests', their aim is simply to create a European nationalism. Their quarrel with those of us who continue to defend national sovereignty, therefore, is not one of principle, but one of scale.

Having thus demonstrated that European federalists have, intellectually, a very weak case, it is now time for us to enter the institutional debate; to do that we have to be sure about our arguments. These will be convincing only if they are based on sound principles, so that in the rest of this paper, these principles will first be outlined, and then specific reforms will be proposed.

First principles

The principles on which the institutional proposals are based are the following:

1) The need to protect and increase individual freedom;

2) The need to create the fewest possible layers of government;

3) The need to build on achievements to date;

4) The need to preserve flexibility of structure;

5) The need for checks and balances;

6) The need to guarantee human rights;

7) The need to guarantee peace in Europe;

8) The need to reject imperial or superpower status;

9) The need to preserve national sovereignty.

Let us now examine these principles in more detail.

1) At the heart of all the work of Britain's anti-federalists has been the determination to increase the freedom of the individual to compete politically, socially and economically. We must strive to ensure that he does not become the prisoner of a European bureaucracy; that his economic freedom is not limited by harmonisation for the sake of harmonisation; and that integration takes place only for his greater good and not merely for the sake of integration. These proposals, therefore, will concern themselves with limiting government, restraining bureaucracy, guaranteeing human rights and enhancing peace.

2) It is more or less an axiom of government that the more levels of government that are provided for, the more government and bureaucracy we will get. The idea that government can be redistributed so that the same amount can be spread over more layers is demonstrably false. Hence, the assurances of the federalists, that the creation of a European government would merely entail a transfer of powers to Brussels, leaving correspondingly less government below, are empty of substance. These proposals, therefore, will not involve the creation of any new layers of government. They will attempt instead to rationalise present structures and to inhibit the growth of bureaucracy by controlling the role of the European Commission.

3) The Community has proved itself quite able in the past to develop institutional procedures which are both efficient and appropriate. Examples include the rotating presidency of the Council of Ministers; the right of the Commission to take member states to the European Court; the convention of always trying to arrive at a unanimous decision even when majority voting is allowed for under the Single European Act. These are precedents upon which we should build.

4) The proposals contained in this chapter are based on the situation which pertains in Europe today. They assume that if there is such a thing as a 'European interest' it is either fairly obvious – in which case national governments will be able to deal with it – or it is obscure – in which case the majority votes of a federal parliament are unlikely to illuminate it, since most European elections are fought along national lines. The time may come, however, when European citizens will vote

on genuinely European issues, and will expect a genuinely federal government to take decisions and to be answerable for those to a genuinely federal parliament. That day has not yet arrived. Nonetheless, there has to be room for change if that change is demanded. After all, both Swiss and American history provide examples of states moving from a loose confederation to a more federalist union. These proposals will therefore allow room for change, but not by the imposition of change on member states which prefer the status quo. Flexibility, in other words, must not be a one-way street to federalism.

5) All democratic institutional arrangements require checks and balances to preserve accountability and to prevent the emergence of elected dictatorships. The proposals in this chapter include checks and balances not only to enhance the accountability of the Council, but to check the growth of government and bureaucracy.

6) The need to guarantee human rights complements the need for democratic institutions. But whereas democratic institutions may take different forms to suit national tastes, human rights by definition must be uniform in nature. If rights are rights, then all Europeans have an equal claim to them. It is therefore proposed that the Community should include within its purview the supervision of human rights in member states.

7) The commitment to peace in Europe is surely the *raison d'etre* of the Community. It is therefore proposed to make this explicit and to proclaim the Community a *Friedensbund* (a Confederation for Peace).

8) There is an assumption among federalists that a united Europe 'speaking with one voice' would exercise more influence in the world and would be able to take its place among the superpowers. Apart from the fact that much would depend on what that voice would have to say, it seems evident that this premiss is illusory. Superpower status has not saved the Soviet Union from economic collapse; nor has it saved the USA from unnecessary wars and military commitments merely to safeguard prestige. Japan, on the other hand, has done much better by neglecting defence, foreign affairs, and the striving after international status altogether. Europe would do well to follow her example. Otherwise, the pursuit of world power status is likely to involve unnecessary expense in order to exercise international influence in a variety of spheres, such as Africa and the Middle East. The rejection of federalism would help Europe reject the kind of vain-glorious foreign policy which would all too likely accompany it.

9) National sovereignty is not to be confused with nationalism and

certainly not with aggressive nationalism. It has nothing to do with illiberalism and is at heart a defensive and libertarian concept. It does not imply the superiority of one nation over another. Quite the reverse. It is the legal defence of small nations against aggressive neighbours. It was Poland's answer to Hitler; Czechoslovakia's to Brezhnev; Lithuania's to Gorbachev, and Kuwait's to Saddam. It is to nations in international society what civil rights are to individuals in civil society: their legal defence against superior power. To ask a nation to surrender its sovereignty is like asking an individual to surrender his civil rights. In Europe, historically, the enemies of national sovereignty have always been the enemies of freedom. Nor is national sovereignty to be confused with national irresponsibility – the belief that the nation-state has either the right or the capacity to do anything it desires. That is an illusion. At heart, national sovereignty is a legal concept. It is the authority vested in the government of each state to take decisions on behalf of the people of that state. As such it cannot be shared. In an interdependent world, of course, states may choose to exercise their sovereignty by associating with other states and to do things in common. However, in so doing they do not relinquish their national sovereignty, but merely agree to act jointly in a specific sphere for a specific or unspecific length of time. They always retain the right to put an end to their cooperation with others, even if that right may entail certain political or economic costs. Sovereignty is the right to exercise authority; it is not the ability to avoid consequences.

With regard to the European Community, this means that the United Kingdom, for example, has chosen to exercise its national sovereignty by associating itself with other states in certain institutional arrangements; her decision to do so, however, has not – indeed could not – involve the transfer of sovereignty to others. Constitutionally, sovereignty in the United Kingdom resides with the Queen in Parliament. Hence the work of the European Parliament, the European Commission, the Council of Ministers and indeed the European Court can only have meaning for the United Kingdom so long as Parliament enforces their decisions and retains the right at any time to end that cooperation. The same is true for all the other sovereign parliaments of all the other member states.

Given this situation, it would seem to be desirable to form institutional arrangements in Europe which reflect this basic principle. At present there is a great deal of loose talk about 'pooling' or 'sharing' sovereignty; there are even voices making the mistaken and illogical claim that the European Parliament has developed a sovereignty of its own. This is untrue, but the very fact that MEPs and others believe it means that the European Parliament, if given more powers, would seek to undermine the status of national parliaments and to subordinate them to its pretended authority. I will therefore propose new institutional and budgetary arrangements which will guarantee the status, and delineate the role, of national parliaments.

Proposals

A European Community has developed because European states have recognised that there are certain areas in which they must work together. Cooperation between states is a common experience in international affairs, as the existence of NATO, OECD, UNO, the IMF and many other bodies testify. Even so, the existence of a directly elected European Parliament has caused several Europeans to call for the establishment of a federal (ie. supra-national) government as the logical counterpart to that body. This should be rejected as totally unnecessary. European states are highly sophisticated organs which are already used to operating an enormous range of policies. They do not require supranational supervision. At the heart of the proposals below is the reform of the European Parliament in order to put an end to the centralising dynamic which it creates. In short, it is proposed that Europe should be run with a parliamentary structure which establishes at the outset that sovereignty derives from the individual member states. This is the only way to insert a protective shield between the freedom of the individual and the bureaucratic tendency already all too apparent in Brussels, which treats Europeans as identikit beings to be shaped according to institutional needs rather than personal desires.

A. The European Parliament

Europe needs a parliament. Given the existence of European legislation and a Council of Ministers, it is imperative that a parliament should exist to scrutinise the men and measures involved. Ideally, each national parliament should agree on all legislation first, but in practice this is impossible: hence the need for a common forum. There are many advantages to be gained by the parliamentarians concerned, quite apart from the obvious one of accountable government: the habit of cooperation; increased knowledge of European politics; an awareness of different cultures and values.

Today, alas, the European Parliament has too few powers to act as an effective brake on the European Commission. It has no formal links with national parliaments, little public profile, and ambitions which are undermined by the general indifference of national electorates. Given the self-expanding powers of the Commission, the result is a 'democratic deficit' at European and national levels which is exacerbated on the one hand by the incipient competition between the European Parliament and national legislatures, and on the other by the fact that most politicians of the first rank choose to pursue their careers in domestic politics.

It is therefore proposed to strengthen parliamentary accountability in the EEC and to eliminate the 'democratic deficit' by integrating the parliamentary process at national and Community levels. My proposals fall into a number of categories as follows.

a) Structure By reaffirming the wisdom of the founders of the Community, the European Parliament will be constituted according to the original Article 138 of the Treaty of Rome (1957) and will therefore become an assembly of representatives from national parliaments.

b) Procedure Delegations from each national parliament will reflect the political composition of their domestic legislature according to the procedures selected by the national parliaments themselves. They will be responsible for explaining their actions to their domestic parliaments as a whole. National parliaments will retain the right to elect their European representatives from amongst their members, through internal parliamentary elections every two years. Individual MEPs from national parliaments will vote according to conscience, but will have the right to form 'parties' or blocs with MEPs from other member states. If a majority of any national delegation objects to legislation proposed in the European Cabinet on the grounds that it undermines a vital national interest, and find their objections sustained by a majority in their national parliament, the proposed legislation, even if passed, will not be applicable to the country concerned.

c) Scrutiny of the EC budget Members of the European Parliament will have their powers strengthened by gaining the right to scrutinise the EC budget in detail and to amend or reject it by a majority vote. The European Parliament will not have the right to increase the EC budget without the consent of the EC Cabinet and Council. In order to ensure that all member states contribute equitably, funds for the EC budget will derive from national quotas defined as an agreed proportion of national GDP. (There should therefore be no need for individual national rebates.) Within the framework of the Single European Act, and with respect for national procedures, financial accountability will be consolidated through the establishment, in each member state, of a visible European Community tax to raise the national contribution to the EC budget.

d) Legislation All European legislation must be approved by a majority in the European Parliament. The European Parliament will have the right to censure, by a majority vote, all members of the EC Cabinet. Proposed changes to the Treaty of Union must be approved, in the first instance, by two-thirds of the European Parliament.

B. The European Cabinet

The present Council of Ministers will be given increased status and responsibility by becoming a European Cabinet consisting of one national minister from each member state. The European Cabinet will be permanently resident in Brussels, responsible for proposing and agreeing European legislation, as well as the EC budget.

The European Cabinet will be responsible, in true parliamentary tradition, to the European Parliament, and all EC Cabinet members will be ex-officio members of the European Parliament. Each member of the European Cabinet will also have cabinet status in his domestic government (e.g. Secretary of State for Europe, instead of Secretary of State for Scotland, Wales or Northern Ireland, to use the United Kingdom model as an example). Each national Secretary of State for Europe will serve at the behest of his national government and will be responsible for coordinating the work of the European Cabinet with the work of his domestic cabinet.

The European Cabinet will distribute European portfolios amongst its members under the direction of a rotating President who will make annual 'State of the Union' reports to the European Parliament. The Presidency of the European Cabinet will rotate annually, from amongst its members.

The voting procedure in the European Cabinet will rest upon the principle of unanimity, except for areas specifically designated by the European Council for majority voting. It will sign trade and membership agreements on behalf of the European Union, provided these fall within the competence of the Treaty and are approved by the European Parliament. It will have the right to propose amendments to the Treaty of Union.

C. The European Council (Heads of Government)

The European Council will continue to meet every six months as the highest-level co-ordinating body and will take responsibility for defence and foreign policy of the European Union. European political cooperation will be supervised by Heads of Government and Foreign Ministers working with their own existing Secretariat. The voting procedure of the European Council will rest upon the principle of unanimity save for areas specifically designated for majority voting, which will not include defence, foreign affairs or constitutional amendments.

The European Council will have the right, shared with the European Cabinet, to propose European legislation. Council initiatives will be put to the European Parliament for approval via the European Cabinet. Proposed changes to the Treaty of Union, initiated in the first instance by the European Cabinet, and approved by a two-thirds majority in the European Parliament, will be referred to the European Council for acceptance. If adopted, amendments to the Treaty of Union will only come into force if passed with majority approval of two-thirds of all national parliaments. Countries whose national parliaments reject these amendments will not be compelled to enter into new constitutional arrangements. The European Council will suspend member states found to be in breach of the Peace Protocol.

D. The European Commission

At present, there is no proper European civil service. The nearest equivalent body is the European Commission, whose powers include:

1) the right to review the progress of legislation among member states;

2) the right to negotiate agreements and to administer certain funds;

3) the right to issue directives and regulations and to take member states to the European Court of Justice;

4) the power to initiate and propose legislation.

The first three of these powers are appropriate to the functions of a European civil service. The fourth is not. In a democratically accountable Europe these powers can only be exercised by the European Cabinet. I therefore propose that the European Cabinet will be assisted in its work by the European Commission formed by amalgamating the present Commission, the Council Secretariat and the Committee of Permanent Representatives.

The European Commission, though no longer retaining the right of initiative, will exercise the following responsibilities:

1) To review legislative progress and to take member states to the European Court if they default on their obligations under the Treaty of Union.

2) The right to issue directives, to issue regulations, etc. once these have been approved by the European Cabinet.

3) The right to negotiate treaties and administer funds under the supervision of the European Cabinet.

The European Commission will cease to have any political role (unlike the present Commission), and will not, for example, function as a middleman between the European Parliament and the European Cabinet. Given the increase in powers of the European Parliament, this will no longer be necessary or desirable.

E. The European Court of Justice

Europe needs a supreme court. Given the number of member states, the diversity of their legal traditions, and the vested interests which have to be confronted in breaking down barriers in Europe, a supreme court is indispensable for furthering economic unity. It must also provide a guarantee of civil rights in Europe and help maintain the peace between European states. Democracy depends upon the rule of law, and which rule is law in Europe can only be decided in a European court.

Today, on the other hand, the European Court of Justice has an institutional self-interest in extending the competence of EC institutions and law by adopting a teleogical interpretation of legislation. The Court has also tended to boost the powers of the present European Commission and to neglect the exercise of judicial restraint. In short, there is insufficient provision within the existing treaties to impose a doctrine of *ultra vires* or to encourage the Court to adhere to a strict interpretation of European law. Finally, as presently constituted, the Court has no responsibility for guaranteeing civil rights. My proposals are as follows:

1) The European Court of Justice will ensure the legality of European legislation proposed by the European Cabinet.

2) The Court will ensure that the European Cabinet and European Commission do not act *ultra vires.*

3) The Court will ensure that the Treaty of Union and all European legislation is strictly interpreted.

4) The Court will guarantee the maintenance of human rights in the Community by entrenching the European Convention of Human Rights.

5) Member states failing to uphold human rights will be expelled from the Community on the initiative of the European Court.

F. Amendments to the Treaty of Union Procedure:

1) Changes in the Treaty must originate in the European Cabinet.

2) Proposed changes must be approved by two-thirds of the European Parliament and be unanimously adopted by the European Council.

3) Changes will only come into force if passed by a two-thirds majority of all national parliaments.

4) Member states wishing to retain the *status quo* will not be obliged to accept amendments to the Treaty of Union. The possibility of a multi-tiered Community will therefore be enshrined in the Treaty of Union.

G. Membership of the European Union

1) All democratic European states will have the right to apply to join the European Union.

2) No member state may be expelled save in cases of persistent violation of human rights or violation of the Peace Protocol.

3) Any member state may choose to secede from the Union.

4) Membership of the Union must be approved by a two-thirds majority in the European Council and by a two-thirds majority in the European Parliament.

5) Negotiations regarding new membership will be conducted by the European Commission under the supervision of the European Cabinet.

H. The Head of the European Union

1) The Head of State of the presiding member state of the European Cabinet will act as symbolic head of the European Union for the duration of one year.

2) The Head of the European Union will open sessions of the European Parliament with a speech setting out the objectives of the Union for the forthcoming year.

I. A European Peace Protocol

All member states will pledge themselves never to declare war on one another, enter into hostilities with one another, or sign alliances against one another. Any member state in breach of this Protocol will be suspended from the Union by a declaration of the European Council.

Conclusions

The advantages of these proposals are manifold. First of all, they are logically consistent. The proposed Union is based on the national sovereignty of the member states. Their parliaments send delegations to the European Parliament to question ministers and scrutinise the budget. The budget is made up from national quotas, financed in a manner decided upon by national parliaments, albeit in a way consistent with the integrated market. The fact that members of the European Parliament and Cabinet will be functioning on both European and national levels would correct the democratic deficit. There will also be no rivalry between the European Parliament and the national parliaments. Finally, no single state could dominate the others, or find itself contributing disproportionately financially.

Secondly, inherent within these arrangements are both explicit and implicit safeguards against big government. The dynamic towards ever more centralisation is checked by: the abolition of direct elections; the removal of the right to initiate legislation from the present European Commission; the empowering of the Court of Justice to rule against acts considered *ultra vires*; and the ending of the role of today's Commission as middleman between the Parliament and the present Council. The dual role of both the Ministers and the Members of the European Parliament should also be a disincentive to unnecessary legislative initiatives.

Thirdly, these proposals contain a number of checks and balances. For example, although the right of initiative is restricted to the European Cabinet and the European Council, MEPs will be able to put pressure on Ministers through their national parliaments and governments if they believe initiatives should be taken. Again, although MEPs might wish to block the application of legislation to their own state in order to preserve a vital national interest, this could only be done if both a majority of their own delegation and of the MPs of the state concerned agree to do so. Finally, applicants for membership would have to be European and commend themselves to two-thirds of the European Council and two-thirds of the European Parliament. This would prevent any single state from vetoing an application for membership.

Fourthly, these proposals contain many positive advances. They allow for greater scrutiny of the budget by MEPs and for greater powers for the European Parliament in general. They thus bring real parliamentary government to Europe without undermining the role of national parliaments. They also make human rights a European concern; provide for explicit undertakings to maintain peace in Europe; and provide Europe with a symbolic head.

Finally, they have the advantage of providing a means of attracting to both the European Parliament and Cabinet politicians of the first rank who would view membership of both these institutions as important stepping stones to a successful domestic political career.

These arrangements represent a positive, parliamentary and practical proposal for European Union. They are designed to appeal to the loyalty of all Europeans, and to prevent an unnecessary division between those on the one hand who seek a uniform Europe, and those on the other whose nationalism impedes further cooperation and unity.

Notes

1 *The Times*, p.1, 14 October 1991.
2 Horst Teltschik, 'A new world order' and 'German Comments', *Review of Politics and Culture*, no. 24 (October 1991), pp. 512 and 1011.
3 These facts are not prejudices; the weakness of most contemporary European parliaments emerged in last year's programme of the European Research Seminars of the LSE. The findings are to be published in a special edition of *West European Politics* edited by Professor George Jones.
4 On fraud in the EEC, see Nigel Tutt, *Europe on the Fiddle: The Common Market Scandal*, London, 1989.
5 See the opinion poll reported in *The Times*, 25 October 1991.

PART II

FORTRESS EUROPE?

5 *Richard Howarth*

The Common Agricultural Policy[1]

In most aspects the Common Agricultural Policy (CAP) represents a living example of the realisation of fears for other sectors of the economy if centralisation and harmonisation by regulation were to take place, and if 'Fortress Europe' were to be erected. This chapter explains how the CAP came into being, describes some of its economic consequences, examines the possibility of major reforms, and draws lessons for future policy.

Origins of the CAP

By 1992 the EEC will have had thirty years of experience in the operation of the CAP. Article 38 of the 1957 Treaty of Rome states that: 'The common market shall extend to agriculture and trade in agricultural products.' It goes on to stipulate 'the establishment of a common agricultural policy' and in Article 39 lists the following five frequently conflicting objectives:

a) to increase agricultural productivity...;

b) thus to ensure a fair standard of living for the agricultural community...;

c) to stabilise markets;

d) to provide continuity of supplies;

e) to ensure supplies to consumers at reasonable prices.

Article 40 gives a few hints about the mechanisms a common policy might use ('stockpiling', a 'common price policy', 'one or more agricultural orientation or guarantee funds'), but the Treaty leaves it to the Commission and Council of Ministers to devise, approve, and initiate such a policy. The first Commissioner for Agriculture was Dr Sicco Mansholt, who came from a farming background but was an experienced politician, having been a Minister of Agriculture in successive Dutch socialist governments. He is now revered (or reviled) as the architect of the CAP.

From embarking on his Herculean task, it took Mansholt two hard years from 1958 to 1960 to hammer out agreement in the Council and European Parliament on the basic principles of the CAP. A further two years were required to put into effect detailed regulations on financing the policy and for specified 'commodity regimes': initially for grains (the model on which most subsequent regimes were to be based), livestock products processed from grains (pigmeat, eggs and poultry) and some rather vague rules for fruit, vegetables and wine. So lengthy and gruelling were the final Council negotiating sessions of January 1962 that, according to a Commission press release, they took '23 days during which 140 hours of negotiations, two heart attacks, and one nervous breakdown among the participants took place'. The childish device of stopping the clock to meet a deadline also had to be resorted to.

Yet, in the context of their time, both the principles and the mechanisms which emerged from these heroic labours were foregone conclusions. Unresolved discussions about a common European agricultural market (a 'Green Pool') pre-dated the EEC; they had been going on within the Council of Europe, OEEC, and other forums since 1950. Two opposed schools of thought had emerged. There was a 'protectionist' school, represented by the French, which was inward-looking and seeking to impose a high level of internal agricultural support coupled with stringent import controls; and, on the other side, was the Dutch 'liberal' view, whose chief proponent had been Mansholt himself, which sought to place upper limits on the burgeoning level of agricultural protection in Western Europe.[2]

As the agricultural debate shifted to the EEC it was inevitable that the French school would prevail. The fundamental *raison d'etre* of the Community was to end forever the possibility of another war between France and Germany by binding the two countries together economically. A bargain was struck between the two powers. The industrial market of the Six would be opened to the Germans as long as French farmers were given their heads within a highly managed common agricultural market isolated from external competition. The only reservation which the Germans had was that support for their own inefficient farmers might be less under a common regime than it was under existing policy. For crude party political reasons, Germany's cosseted agriculture had been completely exempted from the free-market policies which characterised the 'economic miracle' of Adenauer and Erhardt. But General de Gaulle would permit no backsliding on the development of the CAP. He linked progress towards the industrial Common Market to progress on agriculture. Without the latter, he would not let the former proceed. It was no coincidence that the abolition of internal industrial tariffs and the erection of the Common External Tariff took place simultaneously with the completion of the main farm commodity regimes in 1968.

Ironically for Mansholt, the only type of common agricultural policy on which he could win political agreement was the one he had previously opposed – a highly protectionist one. It was an amalgam of both the philosophy and the mechanisms of former French (and German) policies which dated back to the protectionist revival of the 1870s. Simple in concept, it was to become hideously complex in its operation. Its four main principles remain in force to this day:

1) a free internal agricultural market with no tariffs, quotas or other barriers to trade;

2) common internal administered farm product prices, determined annually by the Council and maintained by intervention (support-buying) and export subsidies;

3) a common system of external protection which ensures preference to Community farmers, operated by means of variable import levies designed to prevent the 'target price' for EEC farmers from being undercut;

4) common financial responsibility, implemented through the European Agricultural Guidance and Guarantee Fund (normally known by its French acronym FEOGA) which was to be part of the Community's budget.

Following its difficult and protracted birth, further complications and crises were to afflict the infancy of the CAP. The major ones were concerned with the common prices and common finance. The CAP was inherently damaging to the interests of consumers and taxpayers of the EEC, as well as imposing severe burdens on outside suppliers in both the developed and developing world. But the degree of the damage it caused depended, to a considerable degree, on the level of prices of farm products which it imposed.

After two years of discussions and deadlock, agreement on the key common cereal prices was finally reached in 1964, but they were not to come into effect until 1967. Those decisions became the benchmark for all other commodities. Although Mansholt had wanted them to be around the Community average (itself well above the world market level), this proved to be politically impossible. The prices were ultimately pitched much closer to those of the high-price countries (Germany, Italy, Luxembourg) than of the lower price countries (France, Belgium and Holland). Even so, to gain their acquiescence, the farmers of Germany, Italy and Luxembourg had to be given special compensation for three years. The die was cast.

In 1967/68, according to Commission figures, EEC farm prices as a percentage of world prices ranged from 131 per cent for poultry to as high as 175 per cent for beef, 185 per cent for soft wheat and 200 per cent for oilseeds, 397 per cent for butter, and 438 per cent for white sugar. The agricultures of France, Belgium, Holland and Italy were given a terrific boost at a time of unprecedented technological advance which, in itself, was leading to increases in physical output per person employed in agriculture of 5-8 per cent per year in the 1960s and 1970s. The economic consequences were as predictable as the floods that follow a downpour.

Economic consequences

Increased agricultural protection

The new common farm prices, designed to give a reasonable standard of living to poor peasant farmers, greatly increased general agricultural protection above what most member countries would have imposed if left to their own devices. Table 5.1 clearly illustrates this point for five of the original six members (the calculations were not carried out for Luxembourg). The nominal tariff equivalents (NTEs) of price support shown in the Table can be considered as the percentage tariffs which would have to be imposed on imports to yield the same overall protection. In 1956, prior to the formation of the EEC, France, Germany and Italy had relatively high levels of protection, much higher than those of

Table 5.1 Nominal tariff equivalent (NTE) of price support for the main commodities in EEC and some other European countries for 1956 and 1966 (percentages)

	1956	1966
Belgium	6	53
France	18	46
W. Germany	21	55
Italy	16	65
Netherlands	5	37
EEC (5)	17*	52
Denmark	3	5
Ireland	5	3
United Kingdom	31	28
Sweden	26	54

Source: R. W. Howarth (1971) *Agricultural Support in Western Europe*, Research Monograph No. 25, Institute of Economic Affairs, London.

Note: Nominal tariff equivalent is calculated as (Qd-Qw)/Qw
where: Qd = total value of gross output of main agricultural commodities at domestic prices
Qw = total value of gross output of main agricultural commodities at European import (world) prices

* The EEC, as such, did not exist in 1956.

Belgium and The Netherlands which had two of the least supported agricultures in Western Europe, but somewhat lower than those of the UK and Sweden. By 1966, when the CAP was well on the way to completion, world-wide levels of agricultural protection had risen substantially as world prices fell relative to supported prices, but in the EEC as a whole protection had trebled, whilst in Sweden it had doubled, which left the EEC and Sweden with similar protection, but in the UK, Denmark and Ireland it had remained virtually unchanged. In Belgium and The Netherlands protection had risen nine-fold and five-fold respectively.

The first enlargement in 1973, which brought the UK, Ireland and Denmark under the CAP, significantly reinforced this baneful effect. The Netherlands, Belgium, Denmark and Ireland have now come to enjoy and to have an incentive to retain a high level of farm product prices and net budgetary benefits which the EEC's budgetary mechanisms ensure are financed mainly out of the pockets of taxpayers in other member countries, for long principally in Germany and the UK, but latterly also in France.

Comparisons of the levels of support in the EEC and other OECD countries are given in Table 5.2 which covers the period from 1956 to 1990. The top half of the Table continues with the concept of the NTE which was used by the World Bank and other organisations until the early 1980s. This shows that the EEC has maintained a consistently high level of protection which in 1980-82 was 35 per cent above the average for all twenty-four OECD countries (despite being a major component in that average) and three times as high as that of the USA. However, Japan has retained the world's most heavily protected agri-

Table 5.2 Nominal tariff equivalent (NTE) of price support and producer subsidy equivalent (PSE) for the main commodities in the EEC and elsewhere for 1956 to 1990 (percentages)

	EEC	USA	EFTA	Japan	Australia	All OECD
			NTE			
1956	(17)	–	–	–	–	–
1966	52	–	–	–	–	–
1965–74	38	–	62	110	–	21
1975–83	51	–	89	160	–	28
1980–82	54	16	–	144	4	40
			PSE			
1979–81	43	16	–	59	5	32
1984	33	28	–	67	10	34
1985	43	32	–	69	14	41
1986	52	43	–	76	16	51
1987	49	41	–	76	11	50
1988	46	34	–	74	9	46
1989 (est.)	41	29	–	71	10	41
1990 (prov.)	48	30	–	68	11	44

Sources: For NTE: R. W. Howarth (1971) *Agricultural Support in Western Europe*, Research Monograph No. 25, Institute of Economic Affairs, London; R. Tyers, and K. Anderson (1988) 'Liberalising OECD agricultural policies in the Uruguay Round: effects on trade and welfare', *Journal of Agricultural Economics*, Vol. 39, No. 2, May; World Bank (1986), *World Development Report* 1986, Oxford University Press, Oxford.

For PSE: OECD (1987) *National Policies and Agricultural Trade*, Paris; OECD (1989) *Agricultural Policies, Markets and Trade: Monitoring and Outlook*, Paris; OECD (1991) *Agricultural Policies, Markets and Trade: Monitoring and Outlook*, Paris.

culture at almost four times the OECD average in 1980-82. And the EFTA group, which includes the traditionally heavily supported farmers in the small countries of Scandinavia, Austria and Switzerland, has continued with a level of protection which is 75 per cent above that of the EEC.

During the 1980s the OECD has developed a more comprehensive measure of agricultural support which attempts to incorporate not only price support, but all forms of direct and indirect income subsidies and other support. The producer subsidy equivalent (PSE) thus measures the value of all 'monetary transfers to farmers from consumers of agricultural products and from taxpayers resulting from agricultural policy'. The percentage PSE is the percentage of farmers' total current revenue derived from existing policy measures for the products in question. In the case of the EEC about 80 per cent of the total PSE comes from various forms of price support. Nevertheless, the PSE percentages in the lower part of Table 5.2 are not directly comparable with the NTEs in the top part. This is because the NTEs express support as a percentage of (lower) world prices, whilst PSEs are expressed as a percentage of farmers' current revenue valued at (higher) domestic prices. Although PSEs tend to be lower than NTEs, both will normally move in the same direction.

It can be seen that over the past decade the PSE of the EEC peaked at 52 per cent in 1986, and fell to 46 per cent in 1988 and 41 per cent in 1989, not so much because the EEC's institutional prices were falling but more because international agricultural prices increased strongly in 1988 and 1989, largely due to the drought in North America. In 1990 the situation was reversed, when world prices fell substantially, by as much as 25-35 per cent for wheat, sugar and dairy products, and the PSE climbed again to a provisional 48 per cent.

The EEC has persisted in maintaining a PSE percentage well above the American level (an estimated 1.6 times as high in 1990), although the US level itself rose steeply in the mid-1980s. Little wonder that America shares with Australia and New Zealand, which have two of the world's least supported agricultures, a deep grievance against the EEC.

Budgetary problems and surpluses

The CAP has continually absorbed two-thirds or more of the Community's budget and has therefore been the major source of its long-running budgetary problems and wrangles. Table 5.3 illustrates the

Table 5.3 EEC agricultural budget expenditure (FEOGA) 1965–1990 (£m.)

1965	64.6	1978	5,667.7
1966	220.5	1979	6,831.7
1967	338.3	1980	7,031.6
1968	1,287.7	1981	6,356.1
1969	1,609.0	1982	7,311.1
1970	2,948.4	1983	9,593.0
1971	2,194.9	1984	11,060.1
1972	2,344.2	1985	12,078.5
1973	2,618.3	1986	15,344.3
1974	2,417.9	1987	16,662.8
1975	2,712.1	1988	18,138.1
1976	3,657.4	1989 (est.)*	17,371.1
1977	4,489.4	1990 (prov.)*	19,203.9

* For these years the figures are net of producers' contributions to FEOGA

Sources: 1965–79: EEC Commission (1981) *The European Community's Budget*, European Documentation Periodical 5/1981, Luxembourg. 1980–83: House of Lords (1985) *The Reform of the Common Agricultural Policy* (HL237), HMSO, London. 1984–87: EEC Commission (1988) *Green Europe No. 42*, Brussels. 1988–90: OECD (1991) *Agricultural Policies, Markets and Trade: Monitoring and Outlook*, Paris.

Note: Exchange rates (£/ECU) from *The Economist Diary 1991* , various issues.

escalation of FEOGA over the past twenty-five years.

As agricultural production grew faster than demand, surpluses of cereals, dairy products, sugar and wine – the mountains and lakes – had emerged by the late 1960s. As new commodities came under the CAP, the cost of FEOGA quadrupled between 1967 and 1968 and then increased a further 22 per cent in 1969, by which time the annual expenditure of the Fund, predominantly for intervention purchases, had risen to £1.6 billion out of a total budget of some £2 billion.

With British entry, a large new market for the surpluses became available. It happened to coincide with the temporary commodity boom of 1972 to 1975, during which the prices of most farm products rose sharply on world markets so that between 1970 and 1975 the cost of FEOGA stabilised at around £2-3 billion per year. Thereafter it has rocketed. After doubling between 1975 and 1978, it doubled again by 1985 when it reached £12 billion. In 1986 the cost of FEOGA rose by more than a quarter to £15.3 billion. The CAP was now out of control. Surpluses rose alarmingly as outlets on the world market even at give-away prices became more difficult to find. By the end of 1986 record amounts of butter (1.3 million tonnes), cereals (14.7 million tonnes), and beef (672,000 tonnes) were bulging out of the intervention stores, despite almost 40 per cent of FEOGA being spent on export subsidies.

Part of the reforms of 1988 (mentioned shortly) were plans to reduce these surpluses by a vigorous policy of increased export subsidies regardless of the external consequences. By early 1990, helped by the fortuitous climatic occurrences of 1988, the mountains had been reduced to molehills. But since then they have swollen once more as the reforms have proved to be ineffective. Across Europe in May 1991 refrigerated stores, including ships with chilled holds moored off Cork in Ireland, and silos were once more overflowing with 800,000 tonnes of dairy products, 800,000 tonnes of beef and 19 million tonnes of grain. By the end of September intervention stocks of beef (865,000 tonnes) were at a record level.

The provisional FEOGA budget for 1990 was over £19 billion (net of producers' contributions). For 1991 the estimate of the gross bill was in excess of £22 billion, and without a change of policy a further substantial rise is anticipated in 1992. Divided amongst the 9 million persons employed in EEC agriculture, the 1991 figure works out at £2,420 per head, equivalent to a bill of £66.92 for every man, woman and child in the 329 million population as a whole.

It should be remembered that the arguments over who should pay; who were the main beneficiaries; how the budget should be controlled; from what source and by which yardsticks contributions should be raised, had rumbled on through the 1960s. They were the main cause of the French walk-out from the Council of Ministers in June 1965, followed by the Luxembourg Accord of 1966 which (to mollify the French) gave any member the right of veto over Council decisions if it considered its 'vital interests' were at stake.

The arguments were temporarily resolved in the agreements on what were to become the Community's three 'own resources' (the revenues from agricultural import levies, from customs duties on industrial goods, and from a maximum of a 1 per cent rate of a notional VAT levied on a common basis) which were reached at the same time as the decision to reopen negotiations for British entry at the Hague Summit of December 1969. Britain's membership from 1973 was to lead to repeated disputes about the cost of the CAP and our own budgetary contribution.

At Mrs Thatcher's insistence, one-off refunds of part of Britain's net annual contribution of then around £1 billion were given to us each year from 1980 to 1984. Following the Fontainebleau Summit (June 1984), Britain was given an automatic rebate of two-thirds of the gap between Britain's VAT payments and EEC expenditure in this country, in return for allowing the Community to raise the maximum notional VAT rate to 1.4 per cent from 1986 – mainly to finance profligate agricultural expenditure under the CAP.

But by 1987, even these increased revenues were insufficient to meet rapidly rising expenditure, and the Community faced bankruptcy (or, at least, being unable to meet its commitments), which was only staved off by 'non-reimbursable loans' (i.e. handouts) from member states' exchequers. In February 1988 the Brussels Summit finally agreed on an additional new resource for the Community from 1989 based on a complex formula related to GNP and 'VAT assessment basis', which seems to mean that the maximum available will be roughly equivalent to a 2.2 per cent VAT rate instead of the previous 1.4 per cent. On that occasion the UK had some success in linking the increased resources to some new curbs on the CAP. Since then, however, Britain's net annual contribution has fluctuated from around £1 billion in 1988/89, to close to £2 billion in 1990/91; on Treasury estimates it is expected to fall by 44 per cent to £1.05 billion in 1991/92 before rapidly trebling to £2.87 billion in 1992/3 as a result of adjustments made for inaccurate forecasts in previous years. Britain is currently paying a similar amount to that paid by France, which only became a net contributor in the late 1980s, but only a third of Germany's net payment.[3]

The burden on taxpayers and consumers

Over the years the cost of the CAP to the Community's taxpayers and consumers has been well documented. On estimates published by the National Consumer Council the CAP budget for 1987 cost every man, woman and child in the EEC £60 in that year. National agricultural policies (outside the CAP) which remain for certain commodities, for structural subsidies, for research and advice, and numerous other items probably cost them a further £60 each.[4] In addition to this cost, as taxpayers they paid higher food prices for products covered by the CAP than they would have paid under free agricultural trade. The result of complex calculations by OECD for 1984-86 is an additional £122 per head per year.[5] In total the CAP has been costing each of us some £242 a year. Thus a typical European family of four bears a total burden of almost £1,000 per year or above £18 a week: a burden which is disproportionately heavy for the poorest families which spend the highest fraction of their incomes on food and on those foods, cereals, sugar, and dairy products, which the CAP taxes most heavily. According to Harvey (1991), the burden of the CAP on consumers is roughly equivalent to a 15 per cent VAT on food.[6] A British study from the Institute for Fiscal Studies relating to 1980 estimated the impact of the CAP as a tax on gross household income as being between 6.6 per cent for the poorest households and 2.9 per cent for the richest – averaging 4.5 per cent on all households.[7] Since then the burden of support has escalated considerably further.

Over the past decade a substantial body of literature has built up which documents increasingly sophisticated attempts by economists (mainly employed by international organisations and national governments) to model and to calculate the economic costs and benefits of agricultural support in general and of the CAP in particular. The methodology and results of many studies were reviewed in a most helpful report for OECD by Winters (1987)[8] and in a later special issue of *OECD Economic Studies* (1990).[9] The sophistication of the methods employed, the years studied, the number of products covered, and the assumptions made vary considerably; but the results bear striking similarities. First, all point to the increased instability of world agricultural markets caused by present agricultural policies which use the market as a dumping-ground for surpluses, rather than as a properly functioning allocation system for efficiently-produced supplies. Second, all point to the concealed burden on consumers of the CAP (and other national policies) because they are forced to pay much higher prices for farm products than they would under free trade. Over the past decade this burden of the CAP has remained well in excess of the cost to taxpayers. On OECD's 1990 figures the total transfers associated with CAP and national policies work out to £47.8 billion from consumers and £27 billion (net of budget revenues) from taxpayers, making a total of some £75 billion.[10] The average burden on European consumers is therefore 76 per cent higher than that on taxpayers. In the case of the UK, the most recently available estimates show that consumer costs are 60 per cent higher than taxpayer costs, reflecting the above-average budgetary burden borne by the UK.[11]

A third common strand in these studies is that all point to the inefficiency of current agricultural policies in transferring income to farmers. In nearly every country the gross benefits received by farmers are much lower than the gross costs to consumers and taxpayers. The various estimates for the CAP, based on differing assumptions, show that for every £1 contributed by consumers and taxpayers, farmers receive between £0.76 and £0.53 (i.e. a cost/benefit ratio of between 1.3 and 1.9). The National Consumer Council (1988)[12] quotes a mid-range figure of £0.62. In Britain the total cost of support has been consistently double or more the gain to British farmers. This shortfall arises partly through the higher prices for net food imports into Britain from fellow EEC members, and partly through the budgetary mechanisms which ensure the transfer of funds from countries which are net importers of food (the UK and Germany) to those which are net exporters. In addition, up to 20 per cent of the expenditure of FEOGA has gone on storage costs of surpluses, whilst administration absorbs another 5 per cent. Moreover, reports from the European Parliament suggest that a scandalous 10 per cent or more of FEOGA expenditure (£2 billion or more) is fraudulently expropriated, mainly by 'middlemen' making bogus claims for export subsidies to third countries and for monetary compensation amounts on intra-Community farm trade.

On top of these 'deadweight losses', current estimates[13] suggest that as much as a further 25 per cent of agricultural support expenditure is wasted in overcoming the depressing effects (mainly via export subsidies) on world market prices of policy itself. In other words, world market prices would be higher under free trade, although still well below present supported prices. An estimate for England and Wales[14] has put the fall in the prices of the main farm products under free trade at 32 per cent overall, ranging from 40 per cent for livestock products, to 32 per cent for milk and 22 per cent for cereals.

Figure 5.1 illustrates the inefficiency of the CAP in providing gross assistance to farmers. It shows that out of every £100 of commodity support paid for by consumers and taxpayers, farmers receive only £40, the remaining £60 being 'wasted'. A direct income support system which paid taxpayers' money directly to farmers might be more costly to administer, say 10 per cent of the total cost, but would be far more efficient in that 90 per cent of it would go straight to farmers.

Farmers' incomes

Although the EEC was formed in the shadow of post-war European food shortages and one of its original main aims was to increase self-sufficiency, the primary objective of the CAP has long been to raise and to stabilise farmers' incomes. This reflected the widely-held view of the 1950s, based on the experience of the 1930s, that without intervention farm incomes would fluctuate widely, and would on average be

Figure 5.1 Efficiency of present CAP compared with direct income support: the destination of £100 of farm support

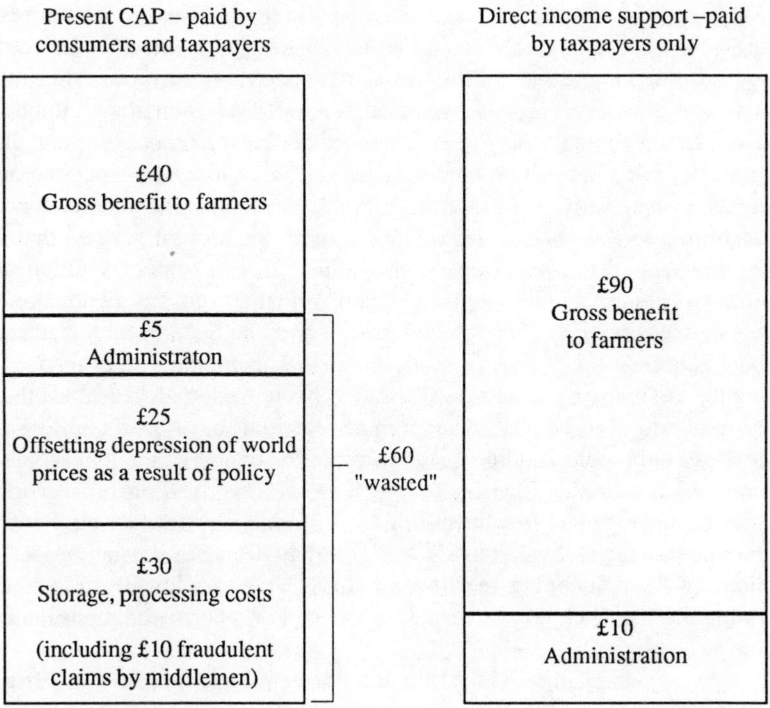

low both absolutely and in relation to other incomes.

By the early 1980s it had become clear that such a view was quite simplistic. It is impossible to generalise about farming and its income. There are variations due to geographical area, type of farming, size of farm, and business performance. Farming embraces both very poor and very rich people. Moreover, many farmers have other sources of income which can result in relatively high total incomes. At least a third of EEC farmers had earned income from other gainful activities, according to the 1983 Farm Structure Survey (Gasson, 1988).[15] In the UK the figure was 31 per cent and in Germany 43 per cent. Blanket forms of price support for all farmers, regardless of income, are therefore inappropriate and wasteful. When 80 per cent of output is produced by 20 per cent of farmers, and support is linked to units of output, it is obvious that the bulk of the support will end up in the pockets of the small number of larger (and generally more prosperous) farmers. In brief, the CAP system has been a mechanism for transferring money from poor urban consumers to wealthy rural producers. It is a regressive system which the founding fathers could never have intended.

Apart from the inefficiency of the support system in transferring revenue to farmers already referred to, much of the gross gain by farmers is eventually absorbed by other factors of production and is therefore not a net gain to farm incomes. Economic theory teaches that normally a subsidy will ultimately be allocated to factors of production according to their elasticities of supply, with the biggest gain going to factors with the lowest supply elasticities. Land, which is fixed in amount, obviously has the lowest supply elasticity of any factor used by agriculture. Land values and rents have, in fact, been the main beneficiaries of support. In money terms, British land values reached eighty times their pre-war level in 1983, having risen at five times the general rate of inflation. The ultimate recipients have been those who owned land before and during the increase in support of the 1950s, '60s and '70s, including owner-occupiers as well as landlords. Tenant farmers have generally gained little. And farmers as a whole have suffered declining real incomes since the early 1970s, as increasing proportions of their declining real revenue have been swallowed up by the rising costs of fuel, labour, machinery, chemicals, borrowed money and rents.

Indeed, when adjusted for inflation, the economic indicators of British farming over the past two decades make sorry reading, as Table 5.4 shows. Taking 1970 as a base, real farm product prices rose by only 19 per cent by 1976 even with the world commodity boom and EEC entry to boost them. They had fallen back to their 1970 level by 1979, since when they have fallen to 64 per cent of it in 1989. Real farming income peaked in 1973 and has been on a downward trend ever since, reaching 38 per cent of its 1970 level by 1989. Rents, which are always lagging well behind trends in profitability of farming, have consistently remained ahead of inflation since 1979, falling back from their rapid increases in the early 1980s to 113 per cent of the 1970 figure by 1989. Land values have performed best of all. Real land values peaked in 1973 at 235 per cent of their 1970 level, which anticipated huge increases in farming profitability under the CAP which were never realised. They fluctuated widely during the 1970s and early 1980s, but

Table 5.4: Some comparative indices affecting UK agriculture (prices, incomes, land values, rents, and input costs) 1970-1989, all in real terms (1970=100)

	Farm product prices	Farming income	Land value (England and Wales)	Rents (GB)	Feeding-stuffs costs	Fertiliser costs	Fuel costs	Farm machinery costs	Farm labour costs	Purchasing power of the £
1964/65–1965/66	109	96	120	86	100	99	102	104	83	128
1970	100	100	100	100	100	100	100	100	100	100
1971	96	103	97	98	88	100	98	99	102	91
1972	93	102	207	99	99	110	97	101	110	85
1973	112	128	235	94	137	120	107	100	120	76
1974	108	91	169	87	123	124	122	105	134	65
1975	107	91	114	80	106	163	118	109	133	52
1976	119	102	135	83	122	139	126	116	137	45
1977	107	87	158	86	117	139	129	123	129	39
1978	102	80	195	95	106	124	120	128	136	36
1979	100	66	231	101	106	132	132	127	141	32
1980	89	51	190	100	96	123	148	123	145	27
1981	88	60	169	104	92	126	161	118	142	24
1982	87	70	166	110	89	123	172	117	142	22
1983	87	53	178	117	92	116	183	117	147	21
1984	83	77	161	123	90	114	179	127	148	20
1985	78	39	150	125	83	113	184	132	150	19
1986	75	49	125	125	79	97	139	133	148	18
1987	72	49	139	123	75	84	128	131	148	17
1988	68	35	157	117	74	81	114	124	146	16
1989	64	38	n.a	113	73	84	111	130	143	15

Sources: Compiled and calculated from: *Annual Abstract of Statistics* (various); *Annual Review of Agriculture* (various); MAFF (1990) *Agriculture in the United Kingdom, 1989*. Burrell, Hill and Medland (1986) *Statistical Handbook of UK Agriculture*, Wye College, Ashford. Marks and Britton (1989) *100 Years of British Food and Farming*, Taylor & Francis, London. Originally published in: R.W. Howarth (1990), *Farming for Farmers? A Critique of Agricultural Support Policy* (2nd edn.), Hobart Paperback No. 20, Institute of Economic Affairs, London..

definitely fell in the late 1980s due to actual and threatened cuts in support. In 1988 and 1989 they rose with the housing boom, ending at around 60 per cent above the 1970 level.

The CAP has not only been extremely costly and wasteful, but also largely futile! Even the European Commission has at last admitted as much: 'In recent years farmers do not seem to have benefited from the increasing support which they have received'(*Green Europe*, 1987, p. 217). By the mid-1980s a general academic consensus had been reached that Ricardo was right when he wrote: 'corn is not high [in price] because a rent is paid, but rent is paid because corn is high' (*Principles of Political Economy and Taxation,* 1817). This view that the gross benefits of high product prices are absorbed by increased rents and value of land has been emphasised in numerous other studies by such respected bodies as the Australian Bureau of Agricultural Economics (1985), the World Bank (1986), OECD (Winters, 1987), and the National Consumer Council (1988).[16] It is also a main plank in the argument of the leading American agricultural economist, Professor D. Gale Johnson, in the recent second edition of his classic study, *World Agriculture in Disarray* (Macmillan, 1991).

The impetus for reform

The chorus of complaint

New voices have steadily joined the chorus of complaint about the CAP. It will suffice to mention two increasingly vociferous groups. First, environmentalists have grown rapidly in sophistication and in numbers: the Royal Society for the Protection of Birds now has three times as many members as the National Farmers' Union. They object, among other things, to the removal of hedgerows and ditches; the increased use of artificial fertilisers, herbicides, chemicals and drugs; the drainage of marshes; the 'reclamation' of hills and woods; and the excessive use of fuel-guzzling machinery. Yet all these developments that are claimed to be damaging to flora and fauna, to sustainable agriculture, and to human wellbeing, have been encouraged by the perverse incentives of artificially high prices and outright subsidies.

Second, macro-economists who have studied the impact of the CAP on the EEC economy and its knock-on effects on world agricultural trade and the economic development of the Third World (Winters, 1987; Moyes, 1986)[17] have concluded that in all these respects the consequences are damaging.

By attracting additional resources into agriculture which would have had more productive uses elsewhere in the economy, 'the CAP has led to massive misallocation of resources in the EC economy' (National Consumer Council, 1988). Moreover, high food prices have caused higher wage claims which have made more difficult the conquest of inflation, worsened the competitive position of the whole economy, and led to increased unemployment. The annual aggregate losses to the EEC could amount to as much as 1 per cent of both GNP and employment. An Australian study by Stoeckel (1985)[18] puts the loss of jobs in the EEC non-agricultural sectors at between 400,000 and 1 million.

Internal pressures

These damaging results have naturally led to pressure for reform from many quarters. Indeed, reform of the CAP has been on the agenda of the EEC for a long time. At the very moment it came to maturity in 1968, Mansholt realised that his creation had become a monster with a voracious appetite for other people's money. He returned to the drawing-board and started afresh. In December of that year he put forward his final Mansholt Plan entitled *Agriculture 1980* – a programme for the decade 1970 to 1980. Over the period the whole emphasis of the CAP was to switch away from price support towards structural reform, including the retirement or retraining of elderly and uneconomic farmers, the amalgamation of small-holdings into economic farming units, and the conversion of marginal farmland into other uses. Half of the Community's farmers and farmworkers would have to leave the land, and an area the size of Belgium be taken out of agriculture.

Not surprisingly, the 10 million farmers and farm workers, and the politicians who sought their votes, did not take too kindly to such a rational approach. The Mansholt Plan was too radical and ahead of its time. But, although its inevitable fate was to lie in a pigeon-hole, it has formed the blue-print for a stream of plans for reform which have followed it over two decades up to and including the Commission's radical Green Paper, *Perspectives for the CAP* (1985), and the actual modest reforms which the Council was forced by the budget crises (and British insistence) to adopt at the Brussels Summit in February 1988. These include:

1) a limit on the annual rate of increase of FEOGA; from 1989 for four years, FEOGA Guarantee Section expenditure growth should be limited to 74 per cent of the annual GNP growth rate of the EC;

2) various methods of back-door price cuts, for example, through limitations on intervention buying, and maximum guaranteed quantities (or 'stabilisers') on which the full support prices will be paid;

3) a doubling by 1993 of moneys allocated to structural reform which covers payments for 'set-aside' of arable land, extensification grants, and an early retirement scheme for 'main occupation' farmers over the age of 55.

Many were sceptical about whether or not these reforms went far enough and whether they would actually be implemented with full rigour. Past experience was not encouraging. Previous attempts at price restraint in the early 1980s were largely unsuccessful, and even when the institutional prices of farm products were reduced or frozen, manipulations of the Byzantine 'green money' system reduced or nullified their impact in many member countries. For example, the general freeze on farm prices agreed in April 1989 was offset for British farmers by a significant devaluation of the 'green pound' – the rate of exchange that is used to convert the common prices denominated in ECUs into the national currency. As a result, UK farmers' incomes were estimated to be increased by £155 million in the following year.

Nevertheless, the political necessity for high levels of farm support is declining as the agricultural population itself declines and changes. The decline of the already relatively small agricultural workforce in the UK is well known – from 8 per cent of the total workforce in 1900, to 4.2 per cent in 1960, and to only 2.1 per cent in 1990. Similar rapid reductions have occurred in continental Europe. The farming population of the original Six fell by one-third between 1958 and 1968 from 15 million to 10 million. Since then it has more than halved to below 5 million in 1989. The agricultural workforces of France and Germany are now down to 6.4 per cent and 3.7 per cent respectively of their total labour forces.

Almost 60 per cent of the Community of Twelve's present agricultural labour force of 9 million persons is now concentrated in the Mediterranean countries of Italy, Greece, Spain and Portugal. Apart from Ireland, where 13 per cent of the labour force is still in agriculture, the political strength of agriculture in Northern Europe is ebbing rapidly, particularly where it has traditionally been the strongest. Having joined in 1981, Greece became fully integrated into the CAP from the beginning of 1986. Spain and Portugal have been given much longer transitional periods of ten years (from 1 January 1986) to integrate their agricultures into the Community. The full impact of the Mediterranean time-bomb which is ticking over the CAP will not, therefore, be felt until 1996. But Spain especially, with the Community's second biggest agricultural workforce after Italy's, has tremendous agricultural potential, and both countries require massive structural adaptations in order to modernise their agricultures. Will the other Community countries really be willing to shoulder the costly budgetary burden of applying the present CAP to the product prices and backward farm structures of these countries? In particular, will France? It is doubtful.

One of the main arguments in favour of present agricultural policies used to be that they helped to maintain the rural population. In most areas rural depopulation is no longer a threat even though the farming population has declined. Throughout the prosperous parts of Europe there is an increasing new migration to the countryside, which is not necessarily popular with its present inhabitants, but which they are powerless to prevent. The formerly abandoned farms of the Dordogne are being reinhabited by retired people, holiday-makers, and those who can use the revolution in information-technology to work from home. In the UK these factors, and improved road and rail communications, have already had their impact on the West Country, East Anglia, North Yorkshire and Cumbria, and are now spreading into Wales and the Scottish borders. All these are areas where properties used to be valued for their agricultural potential alone. They are now more often valued for their residential and development potential. The new arrivals are not sympathetic to the CAP and its consequences.

International pressures

As was shown earlier, the EEC is not alone in maintaining agricultural support; the USA has a lower level and Japan a much higher one. But the ripple effects of agricultural protection have spread far wider than the economies of the EEC, the USA and Japan. As world agricultural markets have decreased through oversupply, the major exporters – the EEC and the USA – have fought to maintain their shares of shrinking trade by increasing their export subsidies. 'In 1987, for example, the cost of wheat export subsidies to the EC reached 140 ECUs per ton or more than twice the world price at that time' (Commission, 1988).[19] The consequences for the nations which are smaller commercial agricultural exporters, and which cannot afford such luxuries as export subsidies, have been obvious. They have had to slash their export prices to unprofitable levels. Their common problems led to the formation of the 'Cairns Group' of four smaller developed countries – Australia, New Zealand, Canada and Hungary – plus ten low-cost developing countries who joined forces in 1986 to press their case for world-wide reductions in agricultural protection.[20]

The relationship between the CAP and the problems of the less developed countries (LDCs) is not a simple one about which it is possible to generalise. First, many of the problems of LDC agricultures are self-inflicted through the ruination of land by deforestation and the neglect and over-taxation of traditional agriculture usually by state marketing boards. This is done mainly out of the desire to provide cheap food for the politically volatile urban masses. (For a more detailed exposition of this argument see Roche, 1986).[21] Second, in the last twenty years many LDCs have become importers on a large scale of dairy products, cereals and sugar through food aid and imports at low concessional prices or at market prices which have been depressed for the reasons given above. If the EEC, the USA and others were to abolish or reduce agricultural protection, surplus production would fall and world prices would rise to the detriment of such countries. They include the Middle Eastern countries, many rich in oil, which would lose out in dairy products, cereals, meats and sugar, but also Mexico and Venezuela in dairy products, South Korea, Nigeria and Mexico in cereals, and Indonesia, Mexico and Nigeria in sugar.

In the short run, the loss or extra cost of imports to such countries might outweigh the gains of increased agricultural exports at higher prices to other LDCs like Brazil, Argentina, Zimbabwe and Chile. This was the conclusion of an Oxfam study (Moyes, 1986).[22] It depended heavily on some unrealistic assumptions but it does reinforce the argument for a gradual withdrawal of protection by developed countries to give the LDCs breathing time in which to build up their own agricultures and to reverse their own self-damaging policies.

Nevertheless, with the exception of the oil and mineral producers, most LDCs will achieve economic progress only by improving their own agricultures in order to reduce dependence on food imports and to earn foreign exchange from food exports. In short, 'trade not aid' remains a valid slogan. As Enoch Powell (*Spectator*, 9 June 1984) rightly put it, there is the 'paradox that we starve those countries precisely by refusing to buy food from them, when food production for export is their only access to wealth and to international purchasing power'.

The Uruguay Round of the General Agreement on Tariffs and Trade (GATT)[23]

The force of the arguments against the CAP and other current agricultural policies had become so strong and so widely accepted that the Cairns Group, the USA and the World Bank joined together in 1986 to press the case for liberalisation of world agricultural trade at the GATT round which began in Uruguay. The USA made the specific proposal that all trade-distorting agricultural subsidies and protection should be abolished by the end of the century.

Agriculture had proved such a thorny issue that it was put on one side in the GATT rounds of the 1960s and 1970s, but this time America was serious, and along with the Cairns Group linked progress in agriculture to further progress in liberalising the multifarious non-tariff barriers to industrial trade and trade in services, and trade-related aspects of intellectual property rights.

The European Community rejected the American 'zero-option' and less radical proposals by the Cairns Group, and stalled the whole talks by refusing to come up with any satisfactory counter-proposals on agriculture. Eventually, in April 1989 all parties, including the EC, agreed that 'the long-term objective is to establish a fair and market-oriented agricultural trading system'. A year later the Community was still unforthcoming on specific proposals. In an attempt to break the deadlock, the chairman of the negotiating group on agriculture put forward three main proposals in early July 1990. On domestic support he recommended commitments to reduce support on the basis of an 'aggregate measure of support'. On border protection, reductions would be negotiated through a process of 'tariffication' of all present methods of protection. On export subsidies (the main bone of contention) it was suggested that they be reduced more than in the other areas.

These proposals were endorsed by the G7 leaders at the Houston Economic Summit later that month who reiterated the objective, agreed in April 1989, of 'substantial, progressive reductions in support and protection of agriculture'. Soon afterwards the USA and the Cairns group proposed that, over ten years, domestic support and border protection be reduced by 75 per cent, and export subsidies by 90 per cent. Eventually, a matter of weeks before the December ministerial meeting of GATT in Brussels, the Community made a totally unacceptable counter-offer to cut domestic support by 10-30 per cent over ten years from the (high) 1986 level, but with no specific commitments on either border protection or the crucial export subsidies.

With the EC prepared to go no further, the GATT talks broke down at the Brussels meeting of December 1990. Despite the fact that the EC had still not agreed internally on reforms to the CAP proposed by Agriculture Commissioner, Ray MacSharry, the GATT negotiations were formally resumed in Geneva at the end of February 1991. In June President Bush obtained from Congress an extension of his 'fast-track' negotiating authority for another two years until early 1993. But the EC has remained on a slow track which could threaten the whole world trading system.

At the time of writing (October 1991) the EC has failed to agree either on internal support cuts as proposed in the MacSharry Plans MK.I (October 1990) and MK.II (June 1991), or on specific new proposals for GATT. The only causes for optimism have been recent hints that the Germans do not really want to be held responsible for torpedoeing the GATT round with the potential adverse consequences for German industrial exports, and that the French are contemplating standing up to their vociferous and violent farm lobby by agreeing to cuts in CAP support. It is unthinkable that the EC should jeopardise the tremendous progress made on liberalising world trade in the post-war period for the sake of the 6 per cent of its employment and 3 per cent of its GNP derived from agriculture to the detriment of the remaining 94 per cent and 97 per cent. But there seems no doubt that it will continue to stall up to and beyond the eleventh hour.

Lessons of the CAP experience

The development of a common farm policy and the form which it eventually took were both political inevitabilities of the 1950s and early 1960s. Without a CAP the French would not have taken part in the EEC, which therefore would not have existed at all. But the time and the trauma and the bureaucratic and political effort which it took to bring it to fruition meant that it became exceedingly difficult to change. In the face of all the criticisms and pressures, the bureaucratic inertia and vested interests have been so strong that it took twenty years from 1968 until February 1988 to reach agreement on any sort of meaningful reform. Even so, it is now clear that the agreed reforms have completely failed to control the CAP.

Lesson one is that any policy of subsidy and intervention is extremely difficult to modify or dismantle.

Lesson two is that when a 'Fortress Europe' has been erected, its common battlements have tended to be as high as those of its member with the highest fortress. Those countries which on their own would have reduced protection have been forced to increase it. For many years it has been clear, as Dr Ralf Dahrendorf put it in his 1979 Jean Monnet lecture, that: '(the CAP) is little more than an instrument for Ministers of Agriculture to get for their farmers in Brussels and in the name of Europe what they would *not* get at their national Cabinet tables.'

Lesson three is that the cost of any common policy of subsidy and support will eventually be wildly beyond all original expectations. As a consequence, its finance will become a source of aggravation and bitterness between the members.

This aspect perhaps gives some grounds for cautious optimism. First, interventionists regard the CAP as the one common policy for European integration which has been put fully into effect. This is not true. The common industrial market, which also came into effect in 1968, is arguably the Community's greatest achievement. Moreover, the CAP has never yet fully achieved all its original objectives. Two of the four basic principles mentioned above have never been put into practice.

Free internal agricultural trade has so far continued to be impeded by non-tariff barriers (such as health, hygiene and other regulations which long prevented trade in liquid milk, for example), and since 1969 it has also been obstructed by the monetary compensatory amount border taxes and subsidies of the 'green money' system. This has also breached the principle of common prices, which, on occasion have differed by as much as 40 per cent between Britain and Germany.

Common finance has been achieved for only about half the total cost of agricultural policy. The bulk of structural expenditure, which is now intended to be an increasing proportion of total expenditure, is met by national governments, which also retain a selection of other forms of agricultural policy of their own. The fact that many recent CAP policies are 'optional' also points to the possibility of some further renationalisation of farm policy.

Lesson four is that the achievement and maintenance of agricultural harmonisation by regulation in a Community of twelve widely different countries is well-nigh impossible. The agricultures of the members are so different in geography, history, structure and sophistication that a sensible common policy is unattainable. This must surely apply to other areas of intervention, and *a fortiori* to an enlarged EEC which may well include the membership of, or close association with, the newly liberated countries of Eastern Europe, as well as the EFTA countries which formed closer links with the EEC in October 1991.

Lesson five is that in the increasingly interdependent international community, the EEC cannot afford to allow the CAP to lead to a trade war with the USA and its other trading partners. Liberalisation of world agricultural trade is increasingly recognised to be economically and socially desirable and politically possible. The EEC will be forced to make concessions to these realities by agreeing to significant reductions in agricultural protection in the present GATT round.

Options for the future

The CAP has been regarded by its proponents as the cement which has bound together the edifice of the European Community. To quote Dahrendorf (1979) again: 'It had its place to cushion a massive migration from agriculture to industry. It may have served to balance French and German economic interests. I have yet to see why a CAP is indispensable today in order to advance the European construction.' It has now become more like an attack of dry rot, which insidiously infects both the internal and the external aspects of that edifice. There are four main options for the future of the CAP: i) continuation; (ii) abolition; iii) repatriation; or iv) reform.

Not only is the CAP a constant source of internal friction, it has now become a major impediment to good relations with outside countries and a threat to the world trading order. It has failed in its main objective of raising most farmers' incomes, and the methods of its failure have caused considerable burdens to those taxpayers and consumers who can least afford them. It is obvious from the preceding discussion that there are few people, apart from segments of the farm lobby in some EEC countries, who believe it is right or possible to continue with the present common policy. From all angles the evidence against it is overwhelming. The clear conclusion on the basis of the arguments already put forward is that the CAP, and other countries' trade-distorting support policies, should be abolished, gradually over a period of say seven to ten years, to permit time for adjustment. But we all know that is not going to start to happen immediately, certainly not within the next five years: the vested interests are still too strong. Nor is it likely, as many of us had thought and hoped, that the CAP will collapse under the weight of its own folly. It has proved to be extraordinarily resilient.

Repatriation (returning agricultural policy to the national governments) would be a desirable second best. Let those who want a high level of support keep it, at their own expense (provided that it is 'decoupled' from production and is non-trade-distorting in form), and let those who do not go their own way. This would be likely to reduce the general level of protection in the EEC and at the same time ease the pressure from GATT. It is also the preferred current stated policy of the British Labour Party and would fit in well with the notion of 'subsidiarity' which the EEC has espoused: leaving national governments to do those things which they are able best to do. Again, it would be difficult to gain agreement on this option, but possibly Britain or other countries could unilaterally opt out of the CAP, particularly if they were to rejoin the EFTA countries in the new European Economic Area of which the CAP is not part.

However, unquestionably the most likely scenario is reform. But what sort of reform and how to achieve it?

Possible reforms

The whole history of the CAP is one of lurching from crisis to crisis, with tinkering stop-gap measures to tide it over to the next one. In the past the crises have been over surpluses (high levels of intervention stocks) and their disposal, and the associated escalating budgetary costs. The crisis of 1991 includes these elements again, but with the added pressures of GATT. In order to plan a sensible policy one must have clear objectives. Lack of them has been a major element of past problems. Now the objectives are clearer since they have been articulated in detail in the MacSharry Plans.

Apart from the original one of a 'fair standard of living for the agricultural community', they include:

(i) maintaining the maximum number of farmers on the land;

(ii) helping farmers and rural areas to diversify out of agriculture;

(iii) encouraging 'extensification', including the role of farmers as custodians of the countryside and the environment;

(iv) continuing with the basic principles of a single agricultural market and common financing;

(v) avoiding the build-up of intervention stocks and improving the competitive position of cereals in particular;

(vi) controlling the growth of FEOGA;

(vii) detaching ('decoupling') agricultural income support from production as far as possible;

(viii) ensuring that the EEC recognises its interdependence on the international scene;

(ix) introducing measures whereby production restraints are increased progressively with the size of farm.

There is little doubt that the USA and the Cairns Group would take no exception to and indeed would welcome many items on this formidable menu. Britain would happily go along with seven out of the nine items. Item (i) has never been specifically on our agenda, but it is item (ix) which is the sticking point for Britain, which points out that it would perpetuate the existence of non-viable continental micro-holdings, whilst unfairly penalising the mainly larger British farmers.

There are essentially three traditional avenues for reform which singly or in combination could satisfy most of the above objectives.

Price cuts To be effective they have to be severe (i.e. 30-40 per cent) and can be introduced directly or by the back door through changes in intervention criteria, co-responsibility levies, or maximum guaranteed quantities ('stabilisers') beyond which prices are cut *pro rata.* They need to be phased in over, say, five years to allow farmers to adjust. They are easy to administer and increase consumption and commercial exports, whilst reducing budget costs and competition from imported substitutes. However, they take time to be effective, cause particular problems for those who are over-borrowed and for small and marginal land farmers, and are generally unpopular with most farmers.

Quantitative controls They include marketing quotas (as have existed for milk since 1984); production or acreage quotas (as exist for sugar beet and potatoes); input controls (possibly on nitrogen fertiliser); and taking land out of production by 'set-aside'. They are preferred by some farmers' organisations (for example, the National Farmers Union of England and Wales), can immediately restrain production/sales and reduce budgetary costs of intervention and export subsidies. To be effective they must be compulsory. They also have formidable disadvantages, including problems of negotiation, enforcement, and revision. They are difficult to dismantle, can ossify the pattern of production if not transferable, and, if transferable, confer fortuitous capital value on farmers. They usually maintain high prices to consumers and lead to landlord-tenant disputes. They are inflexible, excessively bureaucratic and turn farmers into servants of the state, as well as perpetuating a high price and high cost support system.[24]

Direct income support This type of policy targets the person rather than the product and has been favoured by agricultural economists for many years.[25] It was also the favoured approach in the Commission's *Perspectives for the CAP* Green Paper of 1985. It is sometimes said that the existing special subsidies for cattle, for sheep and for farm improvements in the 'less-favoured areas' of the EEC are a form of direct income support. But this is not strictly true. They do target particular marginal farming *areas*, but they apply to *all* farmers in those areas and are paid on the basis of the number of head of *livestock* and *not* on the income of the farmer.

A pure direct income support scheme would be a type of social security which could take several forms:

a) A payment to make up the difference between a *base income* (say 50 per cent of average farm income in the country/region, or a fixed amount of, say, £8,000) and the *household income* of the farm family *from all sources*. This would be highly selective and limited to professional farmers only. It would possibly be a disincentive to some farmers who might decide to take life easy, but if the objective was to keep people on the land, it would enable some of those who might be planning to leave to stay. On the other hand, if it was a social approach purely to help the present generation of farmers who, through lack of education or other skills, and with advancing years, would be unlikely to find alternative employment, it could be limited to them and thus would die with them.

b) A social insurance scheme of benefits for professional farmers if their household income fell to more than, say, 25 per cent below the average of the previous five years. The benefit would be limited to providing a base income.

c) A pension scheme for older farmers, say over age 55. This would be limited to those whose main occupation is farming and would be conditional upon them abandoning their agricultural activity. To be effective the payment would have to be sufficiently generous to provide an incentive for them to leave, but it could be limited to the years before they reached the age of 65 when normal pension schemes would take over.

d) A temporary payment of a 'structural' nature for all existing professional farmers for, say, five to seven years during which produce prices were drastically lowered. Such a payment would ease the transition to a market-oriented agriculture. It could either be a once-and-for-all lump sum, or a decreasing annual payment to avoid an abrupt cut-off. For simplicity it could be paid per acre or per livestock unit or per tonne of product in a base period.

The major advantage of direct income support is that it need not involve large government payments to farmers who do not need them. It is efficient in transferring income to farmers without significantly distorting national and international agricultural markets. By being selective it generally costs much less to taxpayers than blanket price support, and it costs consumers nothing. It could be difficult to administer, but not necessarily any more so than other forms of agricultural policy or of social security. But it is the social security aspect which is unacceptable to farmers and makes such schemes profoundly unpopular with them. For some reason it is all right to receive £5,000 from the Ministry of Agriculture for a subsidy on wheat, but not a cheque for £5,000 from the Department of Social Security! And this is why they have not been adopted more widely, although they are economically by far the most sensible form of support.

Desirable reforms

The principal error of the past CAP is that it has relied almost exclusively on one policy instrument, high product prices, to achieve a number of objectives. Theorists of public policy are now generally agreed that 'a necessary (but not sufficient) condition for the reaching of a number of quantitative objectives is that one employs a similar number of policy instruments'.[26] One reason why the MacSharry Plan (June 1991 version)[27] is not all bad is that it proposes a variety of instruments. First, it proposes the abolition of the complex co-responsibility levies and 'stabilisers' which would be replaced by straightforward deep price cuts – for cereals by 35 per cent over three years to approximately £70 per tonne, for beef by 15 per cent. For cereals compensation, payments to all farmers for income loss would be paid according to tonnage produced. To qualify for compensation farmers over 125 acres would have to set aside 15 per cent of their land without set-aside payment. Farmers under 50 acres would be excused the set-aside requirement. This policy would reduce surplus production, export subsidies and long-run but not initial budgetary cost. It would therefore assist in unblocking the GATT negotiations. Second, it proposes increased environmental subsidies, schemes to convert more farmland to forestry, and the provision of early retirement pensions for the 50 per cent of Community farmers in the 55-65 age group. Again, these would all be to the good from the international point of view.

However, although the MacSharry Plan represents a step in the right direction, it contains some major flaws. The main faults of its key proposals are that compensation is linked to future rather than past production, which would be administratively complex and an open-ended commitment which goes against the idea of compensating farmers for changes in past policies; that there is no fixed time-limit on compensation; that 'degressivity' (larger farmers receiving proportionately lower compensation than small ones) is achieved via compulsory 'set-aside' for larger farmers; and that the proposals do not specifically address the two key issues for our trading partners of variable import levies and export subsidies.

A more sensible compensation scheme would take one or more of the forms of direct income support outlined above. It would limit general compensation to a pre-announced fixed period during which annual payments would decrease to avoid an abrupt cut-off at the end. Permanent payments (which MacSharry perhaps envisages) would simply prolong the existence of inefficient micro-holdings at ever-increasing budget cost. There is no clear case for degressivity, but it probably makes the scheme more politically acceptable. If the principle is adopted, it should be implemented by means other than set-aside which, as American experience shows, is ineffective in reducing output and unnecessarily complicates an already complex system. The idea behind set-aside is to decouple support from production, but there is no need for it under a scheme of transitional payments to a market-based agriculture. Degressivity could be more simply achieved by compensating farmers on a decreasing scale of revenue loss, starting at 100 per cent for the smallest farmers and falling to, say, 50 per cent for the largest. Any scheme which took a responsible attitude to the disbursement of taxpayers' money would be limited to the present generation of farmers and would be selective. In particular, the 40 per cent of EC farmers who are part-time should receive special scrutiny. Is there any case for compensating those for whom the farm is not their main activity?[28]

The PEG alternative

Still less desirable, however, are the MacSharry proposals to continue with milk quotas until the year 2000, and to introduce sheepmeat quotas. If it is not politically possible to introduce straight phased price cuts, the 'production entitlement guarantee' (PEG), normally associated with Prof. David Harvey of Newcastle University, provides a more attractive alternative to quantitative controls.[29]

Under this scheme, all other commodity support would be abolished, whether internal or at the border. Farmers would have a preset fixed limit on the quantity of production of different products eligible for support payments. As long as the total eligible production was less than would be produced without support, prices on the open world market would be farmers' main consideration in planning how much to produce. Apart from the obvious benefits to consumers and taxpayers, the CAP budget, and the international market, PEGs could be targeted at particular groups of farmers, and if they were tradeable between farmers could provide a mechanism by which larger or more efficient farmers could compensate smaller or less efficient ones. Indeed, they could be a self-financing buy-out scheme, which would not have the stigma of a direct welfare payment. They could also be used as a cushioning mechanism for support reductions by the government progressively purchasing their tradeable PEG licences from farmers as a compensation for giving up the right to support. Finally, they would be easy to negotiate and monitor through GATT.

The PEG scheme does not immediately restore agriculture to the free market, but free-marketeers should see its advantage over most other systems of support in that it does restore to farm product prices much of their cardinal function of providing signals to producers and consumers, balancing supply and demand, and allocating resources efficiently within agriculture and between agriculture and other sectors of the economy. Yes, it would retain more resources in agriculture than the free market. Yes, we would all have to forego some small amount of income which the free market would give us. However, as a matter of political acceptability, PEG plus some selective and temporary direct income support along with some diversification and environmental subsidies would be the best that could be expected for the time being.

Conclusion

On its thirtieth anniversary the CAP is in deep crisis, as are many of the farmers whom it purportedly exists to help. It has attempted to impose the failed protective French and German agricultural policies on the previously market-oriented agricultures of Northern Europe, such as those of Holland, Denmark, Ireland and the UK, and more recently on the Southern European peasant agricultures of Greece, Spain and Portugal. In so doing it has satisfied none of them, whilst causing serious friction with outside trading partners. Indeed, an unreformed CAP is now the most serious obstacle to the further liberalisation of world trade and is putting the benefits of past liberalisations in jeopardy.

And yet the warning which the CAP provides has done nothing to dampen the appetites of the centralisers, particularly those in the Commission. Britain may have delayed its own adoption of the 'social chapter' at Maastricht, but the 'structural funds', to which it would be committed to subscribe, are proposed to be doubled, with the 'Cohesion Fund' on the way. Mr Nigel Lawson warned of their consequences at Chatham House in January 1989. His words could equally have been referring to the CAP: 'Grandiose attempts to reduce regional disparities by ever-greater resource transfers are likely to be no more successful at the Community level than they have been within individual countries. Subsidising industries and subsidising regions destroys their will to compete and thus their ability to compete.'[30]

Postscript - June 1992

Shortly before this book went to press, agreement on the MacSharry reforms, with some significant modifications, was reached by the Council on 21 May 1992. The key agreement was for a 29 per cent cut in cereal prices by 1995/96.

Degressivity of compensation was abandoned. All cereal farmers, regardless of size, must set aside 15 per cent of their arable area to qualify for uniform compensation, rising to £208 per hectare in 1995/96. Reform of the dairy sector was also abandoned. Milk quotas are to remain until the year 2000 with no proposed changes in quota sizes or milk prices.

If implemented, these will be the most radical reforms of the CAP so far, but are again likely to provide only a temporary palliative for its maladies. Politically they went as far as was possible, as subsequent vehement reactions of French and German farmers showed. Yet it is doubtful whether they will curb the cereal surpluses, whilst is it certain that, in the short term, they will increase the CAP budget. Moreover, the generous size and apparent permanency of the compensation and the absence of specific commitments on export subsidies and variable import levies have made the reforms difficult for the Americans to accept in the faltering GATT negotiations.

Notes

1. This chapter relies heavily on two other publications by the same author: R. W. Howarth, *The Common Agricultural Policy: an Expensive Lesson on the Dangers of Harmonisation by Regulation*, Occasional Paper No. 7, Bruges Group, London, 1990; R. W. Howarth, *Farming for Farmers? A Critique of Agricultural Support Policy* (2nd edn.), Hobart Paperback No. 20, Institute of Economic Affairs, London, 1990.
2. The level of support in Western Europe in the late 1960s is discussed in: R. W. Howarth, *Agricultural Support in Western Europe*, Research Monograph No. 25, Institute of Economic Affairs, London, 1971.
3. Source: *The Economist*, 17 November 1990, p. 43.
4. National Consumer Council, *Consumers and the Common Agricultural Policy*, HMSO, London, 1988.
5. OECD, *National Policies and Agricultural Trade: Study on the EEC*, Paris, 1987.
6. D. R. Harvey, 'The PEG option' in C. Ritson and D. R. Harvey, *The Common Agricultural Policy and the World Economy*, CAB International, Wallingford, 1991.
7. A. W. Dilnot and C. N. Morris,'The distributional effects of the CAP', *Fiscal Studies*, Vol. 3, No. 2, Institute for Fiscal Studies, London, July 1982.
8. L. A. Winters, 'The economic consequences of agricultural support', *OECD Economic Studies*, No. 9, Paris, 1987.
9. OECD, 'Modelling the effects of agricultural policies', *OECD Economic Studies*, No. 13, Winter 1989-90, Paris, 1990.
10. OECD, *Agricultural Policies, Markets and Trade: Monitoring and Outlook*, Paris, 1991, p. 139.
11. Estimates in: R. W. Howarth, *Farming for Farmers? A Critique of Agricultural Support Policy* (2nd edn.), Hobart Paperback No. 20, Institute of Economic Affairs, London, 1990, p. 200.

12. National Consumer Council (1988), *op. cit.*, p. 53.
13. Quoted in: C. Ritson and D. R. Harvey (1991), *op. cit.*, p. 328.
14. Quoted in: D. R. Harvey, *Farming without the Government: What Would it be Like?*, Agricola Paper No. 87/2, Wye College, University of London, 1987, p. 4.
15. R. Gasson, *The Economics of Part-Time Farming*, Longman, Harlow, 1988.
16. Bureau of Agricultural Economics, *Agricultural Policies in the European Community: Their Origins, Nature and Effects on Production and Trade*, Canberra, 1985; World Bank, *World Development Report 1986*, Oxford University Press, Oxford, 1986; L. A. Winters (1987), *op. cit;* National Consumer Council (1988), *op. cit.*
17. L. A. Winters (1987), *op. cit.* A. Moyes, *How Farming in Europe Affects the Third World Poor*, Oxfam, Oxford, 1986.
18. A. Stoeckel, *Intersectoral Effects of the CAP: Growth, Trade and Unemployment*, Bureau of Agricultural Economics, Canberra, 1985.
19. Commission of the EC, *Disharmonies in EC and US Agricultural Policies*, Brussels, 1988, p. 2.
20. The full membership of the Cairns Group which accounts for approximately one quarter of world trade in agricultural products is: Australia, New Zealand, Canada, Hungary, Argentina, Brazil, Colombia, Chile, Fiji, Indonesia, Malaysia, the Philippines, Thailand, and Uruguay.
21. L. Roche, 'Forestry and famine: arguments against growth without development', *Commonwealth Forestry Review*, 65(2), 1986.
22. A. Moyes (1986), *op. cit.*
23. For information on the progress of the GATT negotiations up to the summer of 1991 this section has used extensively: H. Corbet, 'Agricultural issue at the heart of the Uruguay Round', *National Westminster Bank Quarterly Review*, August 1991.
24. For detailed critiques of supply control see: D. R. Harvey, *Milk Quotas: Freedom or Serfdom?*, CAS Study 1, University of Reading, 1985, and A. Buckwell, *Controlling Cereal Surpluses by Area Reduction Programmes*, Dept. of Agricultural Economics, Wye College, University of London, 1986.
25. See for example: B. C. Swerling, 'Income protection for farmers: a possible approach', *Journal of Political Economy*, Vol. 67, April 1959.
26. T. Josling, 'A formal approach to agricultural policy', *Journal of Agricultural Economics*, Vol. XX, No. 2, May 1969.
27. Details of the plan taken from: The Scottish Agricultural College, *Monthly Economic Survey*, Vol. 17, No. 7, July 1991.
28. These points and many others are further developed in : S. Tangermann, 'Reforming the CAP?', *IEA Enquiry*, No. 28, Institute of Economic Affairs, London, February 1992.
29. The most recent discussion of PEG is in C. Ritson and D. R. Harvey (1991), *op. cit.*, Cap. 17.
30. Quotation taken from: *Daily Telegraph*, 16 December 1991, p. 21.

6 *Brian Hindley*

Trade policy of the European Community

The primary characteristic of EEC trade policy is the sulky obstinacy. The EEC is the world's largest trading entity, but it cannot seem to find positive uses for the influence that its mass should bring. It uses its bulk in stubborn defence of its own narrowly-defined interests, without apparent thought for the effects on the world trading system. The state of the world trading system, though, must itself be a major interest of the world's largest trader, not something that an enlightened pursuit of EEC interests would ignore.

In the Uruguay Round of trade talks in the GATT (General Agreement on Tariffs and Trade), for example, the EEC's refusal to contemplate substantial change in the Common Agricultural Policy (CAP) caused a breakdown of what was scheduled to be the final meeting of the Round, in December 1990. The Uruguay Round is intended to remove many blemishes in the structure of the GATT which, whatever its defects, is the world's only safeguard against trade mayhem. With a modicum of imagination, the EEC could have taken the lead in fulfilling the objectives of the Round, given the difficulties of the US administration in the face of Congressional concern with the US trade deficit. Instead, the EEC has been a principal cause of the breakdown and continuing stagnation of the Round.

M. Delors and other members of the European Commission constantly say that the EEC rejects protectionism. But they also affirm the CAP as a foundation-stone of the EEC. The statements cannot be reconciled.[1] The CAP is protectionism. It increases the wealth of a small section of the EEC population at vast expense to the rest. It inflicts great harm on agricultural producers outside the EEC – among them, efficient producers in developing countries and in Eastern Europe.

The EEC's current negotiations with Poland, Czechoslovakia and

Hungary, on the terms of their future association with the Community, provide a clearer test than even the Uruguay Round of the value the EEC places on open markets.[2] The Eastern European countries, released from the external constraints that have prevented free intercourse with Western Europe, now also seek to remove the barriers imposed by the EEC and by themselves. The EEC has a clear interest in the political character of its eastern neighbours, and it can influence that character. The opportunity to trade freely with the EEC will greatly improve the chances that the Eastern European countries will ultimately emerge as prosperous liberal democracies.

Even were the interests of the EEC less heavily engaged, it might be thought to have some moral obligation towards the peoples of Eastern Europe. The bulk of those Europeans had no hand in creating the misfortunes they suffered over the past five decades. To remove the barriers that prevent them from offering their products to Europeans in the EEC (who will themselves gain from such trade) could be seen as a rather minimal response by their very much more fortunate neighbour.

Economic, political and moral considerations all point to free trade with Eastern Europe. A naive observer might therefore suppose that the negotiations with Poland, Czechoslovakia, and Hungary would flow smoothly to that conclusion. Official statements of the aim of the negotiations add to that impression. In principle, it is intended to lead to free movement of goods, capital, labour, and services between the EEC and Poland, Czechoslovakia and Hungary. The crucial words, though, are 'in principle'. The important question is what the exceptions will be in practice. Much of what Poland, Czechoslovakia and Hungary currently have to export falls into categories regarded as 'sensitive' by the EEC, and subject to special protective regimes – for example, agricultural produce, textiles, coal and steel. Even granting these sensitivities, though, one might still think that the strength of the case for free trade in this particular case is such that EEC would find means to relax its protective regimes in favour of Eastern Europe. But these possible thoughts of a naive observer have proved to be – naive. The EEC's negotiation with Poland, Czechoslovakia and Hungary has been blocked by the refusal of the EEC to make substantial concessions in its protection of agriculture, textiles, steel or coal.

What can be made of this? A great historical watershed has been passed. The eastern part of the European continent is in the midst of a vast and unprecedented restructuring, the outcome of which is unknown, but whose course can clearly be influenced by the EEC. And the EEC baulks at permitting additional imports of meat amounting to 0.01 per cent of its total consumption. That is bad for Eastern Europe, but it is also augurs badly for the EEC and badly for the world. If the EEC cannot find the statesmanship substantially to modify its protective policies in this case, or the imagination to devise alternative means of satisfying the clients of its protectionism that would allow freer trade with Eastern Europe, what ability can it have to muster statesmanship and imagination in any other case?

Despite this, the EEC is not yet wholly protectionist. But it is protectionist in too many areas, and too many participants in its decision-making processes favour protection as a 'solution' for their political problems. There is a real danger that the protectionist policies the EEC pursues in some areas will infect the rest of its trade policy. Indeed, that is already happening. Over the past decade, anti-dumping action – in itself perfectly legal – has been developed by the EEC into a protectionist tool. That has been achieved by manipulation of the calculations and distortion of the judgements on which legally-valid anti-dumping action must be based. That manipulation and distortion is as potentially damaging to the GATT as the refusal to limit the CAP. It is discussed in more detail below.

The insensitivity of EEC trade policy to interests and concerns other than its own is not merely a result of the EEC's current inward focus on its programme to complete the internal market by the end of 1992, though that inward focus may exacerbate tendencies that are already present. The underlying attitude of the EEC to trade policy has a much longer history.

The background to EEC trade policy

The European commitment to the central principles of the GATT has always been more tepid than that of the US. That law, not power, should control international economic relations was a US idea. So was its corollary that imports from one source should be treated in the same way as similar imports from another source, and that remedies for trade problems should be independent of the identity of the economy against which they are directed. In the early- and mid-1940s, the US probably was the only country in which such ideas were supported by the administration and a substantial body of opinion at large.[3]

In the conditions of the time, Europeans largely deferred to the US in the matter, but Europeans felt more comfortable with the traditional and opposed view that trade policy should be controlled, not by international law, but by the needs of a broader diplomacy. Current EEC trade policy reflects that feeling. In Brussels, it is possible to detect a sense that the GATT is an irrelevant irritation, tolerated by the EEC only for the sake of good relations with the US. In this Brussels view, the GATT should to be a centre for intergovernmental discussion of trade issues, not a body of enforceable international law.

For many years, the EEC was in the comfortable position of being able to treat the US as the sole keeper of the GATT spirit. The EEC, accordingly, felt able to make as much space for its own preferences and interests as possible within the GATT structure, without thought for the consequences for the international trading system as a whole – it was for the US to take a global view. That attitude is reflected in the fact that whenever possible, the EEC still justifies its trade policy actions, not in terms of the merits of the action, but with the argument that 'the US does it too'. This EEC attitude could work only because those who made US trade policy did think in terms of a global interest. Their identification of it was sometimes suspect, and they did not always – and sometimes could not – act upon their perception of it. But the idea that there is a global interest, which ought to be identified in the process of US trade-policy making, was not alien or offensive to them.

The US, however, has a tradition of schizophrenia in these matters. US trade policy has always mixed blatant and immediate self-interest with acts and proposals that are consistent with a much more broadly-based conception of US interests. And in recent years, the continuing US trade deficit has threatened to tilt schizophrenia into paranoia. The US Administration appears to want to play the traditional US role of principal policy-maker in the international trading system. But that role cannot be sustained if immediate US interest is the sole reference point for US policy. And the Congress is unlikely to welcome actions that it perceives to be contrary to immediate US interests.

The EEC, therefore, may no longer have open to it the soft option of living in a multilateral trading system whose spirit is kept alive by the US, while the EEC contrives adjustments to multilateralism to suit itself. If the US abandons its role as keeper of the GATT spirit, the EEC must either take positive action to preserve the multilateral trading system, or watch it collapse. At the moment, the EEC seems to have opted – more by default than by conscious decision – for collapse. There is a good chance that the Uruguay Round will fail, either in the absolute sense that the Round is abandoned without conclusion, or in the sense that it produces only a cosmetic package of agreements, falling far short of its original intentions, and without actual effect on the world trading system – a figleaf to maintain political and diplomatic respectability.

In a formal sense, failure of the Round will not affect the status of existing GATT law. But it will reduce even further the already low esteem in which the GATT is now held in the EEC and the US. A failure of the Round will thus increase the readiness of the EEC and the US to stretch GATT rules to the limit – and beyond – to achieve their immediate objectives. Neither needs much excuse to raise barriers against Japan. If the Round collapses, EEC protectionists will be able to point to protectionist policies in the US as examples of what the EEC should do, and US protectionists to protectionist policies in the EEC as models for US action. There will be more barriers to trade. The world will be on the way to three trading blocks, and relations between them will be controlled by power – not law. The danger is compounded by recent political changes in the former communist block. The EEC may no longer need the US to defend it. If not, a major constraint on EEC policy towards the US has vanished. The danger is further compounded by the current political state of the EEC. Advocates of a federal EEC often say that they want an EEC that 'can look Japan and the US in the eye'. The comment is a puzzle – why can't we look them in the eye now? – but a clue lies in the tone in which the comment is often made, which suggests that what is sought is an EEC that can look others in the eye while kicking them in the shins. That is alarming. An EEC affirming its identity by aggressive policies towards its trading partners, in an effectively GATT-less world, would be a dangerous beast – except for those who want 'Fortress Europe'.

The case for Fortress Europe

Advocates of an EEC that is closed to trade are thin on the ground. Few openly say that the EEC should retreat into Fortress Europe and pull up the drawbridge. Many, though, say that they support free but fair trade – but define 'fair' in ways that are far from everyday notions. Others say that they support free trade, but that exceptions should be made to support employment; or to maintain technological potential; or to allow an industry a breathing-space while it restructures to meet international competition. The case for an open EEC commands the rhetorical battlefield. The problem is that so many exceptions to openness are widely accepted that an 'EEC open with exceptions' may not be very different from Fortress Europe. 'Free trade but . . .' may propel the EEC into Fortress Europe by accident.

This is not the place to analyse these 'buts'. None of them in fact stand up to rigorous examination. The infant industry argument for protection (or, as it often appears in the EEC, the argument for rejuvenating senile industries by 'temporary' protection) is empty (Johnson, 1971). Overall employment cannot be increased through protection (though employment in one industry can be maintained at the expense of employment in others) (Mundell, 1961; Krugman, 1982). These are arguments that politicians find useful, but that have no economic content.

Those not subject to divergent political pressures should not be contemptuous of the manoeuvres of politicians. The health of a liberal democracy comes into question, though, when the room for manoeuvre of politicians is expanded by false arguments or simple falsehoods. EEC trade policy suffers from a too-easy acceptance of facile arguments for protection. As a result, that policy harms the overall interests of the residents of the EEC, whether considered from a narrow economic perspective or from a broader perspective that takes account of the interests of the EEC in the character of its neighbours and the state of the international trading system.

EEC trade policy has many aspects, and it is impossible to consider all of them here. Instead, I shall illustrate the comments above by reviewing EEC policy in a specific area – that of anti-dumping action, where, as already noted, the EEC has achieved its policy objectives by distortion and manipulation.

EEC trade policy in action: anti-dumping

The story of the EEC's development of anti-dumping action as a protectionist device has two principal strands. One strand starts with Article XIX of the GATT, which allows emergency protection against a sudden surge of a particular class of import, but requires the same treatment of all imports in that class, regardless of their source. In the GATT negotiation that preceded the Uruguay Round (the Tokyo Round), the EEC tried to obtain the consent of other GATT members to an amendment of Article XIX that would have allowed it to invoke Article XIX against 'disruptive imports' – imports from new and efficient suppliers, often located in East Asia – without action against similar imports from other sources. The EEC treated this as a central issue of the Tokyo Round – indeed, it threatened to block all other outcomes of the Round if its proposals on Article XIX were rejected by GATT members. In the event, the EEC proposals were rejected and the EEC did not block the rest of the Round. Instead, the Community turned to anti-dumping action as a means of creating unilaterally the situation that it had failed to achieve through negotiation.

The legal target of an anti-dumping proceeding is always a specific product of a specific company – never, formally, a country. Similar products of different exporters from a particular country often bear different rates of anti-dumping duty. That fact provides a clear protectionist logic for EEC development of anti-dumping procedure. Under Article XIX, different countries cannot be treated differently. Article VI, on the other hand, which controls anti-dumping action, allows discrimination between different companies (subject only to the requirement that they can be found to dump by different margins). Following the EEC's failure to obtain agreement to its proposed amendment of Article XIX, it was probably inevitable that EEC protectionists would shift their focus from Article XIX to Article VI – even if attainment of their ends required some economies with the truth.

The second strand of the history starts with the use of anti-dumping measures as a means of controlling trade between the EEC and non-market economies (NME). When exports of a particular product from an NME were perceived to be 'too high', the problem was typically solved by claims that the product was dumped. To give substance to that claim, the cost of production in the NME was required. But, it was said, costs of production in an NME cannot be directly measured. So they were instead 'estimated' by use of the costs of production of the product in a non-EEC market economy. In a case involving electric motors, for example, the cost of production in Sweden was used as a proxy for costs of production in Czechoslovakia, Hungary, Poland, Bulgaria and Romania (Hirsch, 1988). Sweden and these (then) NMEs have rather different levels of wages, among other things, and this procedure clearly was not designed to provide an accurate calculation of costs. Rather, the procedure was designed to provide a 'legal' means of restricting the offending imports by anti-dumping duties or, alternatively, of providing a basis for a threat of such action to back up a request to the offending suppliers to reduce the volume of exports. In this sense, the EEC's use of anti-dumping to deal with problems of trade with NMEs previewed exactly what was to happen when anti-dumping action was extended to deal with the trade 'problems' created by market economies. In both cases, moreover, great attention is paid to a solemn procedural rigmarole founded on absurdity.

A shift in the direction of using anti-dumping action to deal with market economies (and also NMEs) came with the 'special' case of steel in the late 1970s and early 1980s. The EEC Basic Price System was based on allegations of dumping and, in the case of the EEC, connected VERs (voluntary export restraints) and anti-dumping action. Steel exporters to the EEC who agreed 'voluntarily' to restrict their exports of steel to the EC were rewarded by an exemption from anti-dumping investigation (the outcome of which they might reasonably have thought not to be in doubt). Yet what made steel a special case so far as anti-dumping action was concerned? If the problems of the EEC steel industry with imports from market economies could be solved by that means, why not the similar problems of other industries?

So far, the EEC has used the anti-dumping methodologies discussed below primarily as a means of 'solving trade problems' with Japan and East Asia. Action has been taken against the 'dumping' of, *inter alia*, electronic typewriters from Japan; ball bearings from Japan, Singapore and Thailand; tapered roller bearings from Japan; electronic scales from Japan; hydraulic excavators from Japan; housed bearing units from Japan; photocopying apparatus from Japan; outboard motors from Japan; inner tubes and tyre cases for bicycles from Korea and Taiwan; dot-matrix computer printers from Japan; daisy-wheel computer printers from Japan; compact disc players from Japan and Korea; DRAMs (microchips) from Japan; video cassette recorders from Japan and Korea; video cassette tapes from Hong Kong and Korea; small-screen colour TVs from Korea, China and Hong Kong; photograph albums from Korea and Hong Kong; audio cassettes from Japan, Korea and Hong Kong; and halogen lamps from Japan. Further cases, of course, are in the pipeline. The uninitiated might suppose that this list says something about the trading practices of East Asian exporters. In fact, it says much more about the nature of EEC trade policy.

Anti-dumping tricks

According to the GATT, dumping occurs when the price of a product exported from one country to another is less than the comparable price, in the ordinary course of trade, for the like product when destined for consumption in the exporting country, or is less than the cost of production of the product in the country of origin plus a reasonable addition for selling cost and profit. This may sound straightforward. Reflection might suggest, however, that calculation of the required magnitudes faces formidable practical problems. The EEC exploits that problem in its use of anti-dumping action to provide the selective protection that it sought but failed to get in the Tokyo Round.

Abuse of anti-dumping legislation is hidden in the technical details of dumping calculations – the saying 'the devil is in the detail' might have been invented to describe anti-dumping law. Exposure of abuse involves discussion of those technical details (e.g. Hindley, 1988). Here, to avoid technicality as much as possible, I shall discuss some specific EEC tricks.

Tricks with averages

The first example turns upon the fact that products are typically sold, not at a single price, but at prices that vary with market conditions at the time of the sale and the characteristics of the sale (for example, whether it is a large- or small-volume sale). To obtain a dumping margin, however, anti-dumping authorities must subtract 'the' price in the export market from 'the' price in the home market of the exporter. A natural solution to the problem of obtaining 'a' price is to take an average. The EEC does that, but it does not take simple averages.

First, in calculating the price in the exporter's home market (often referred to as 'the reference price'), the Commission is likely to throw out low-priced sales in the home market of the exporter on the basis that they are unprofitable. The reference price calculated by the Commission will therefore be higher than a simple average of prices of sales in the exporter's home market. Second, EEC methodology treats all export sales at a price above the reference price as if they had been made at the reference price. Thus, the 'export price' as calculated by the EEC is an average of the prices of export sales that are less than the reference price, and the reference price itself: a figure that must be lower than the reference price. Hence, if any export sales have been made at a price lower than the artificially-increased reference price, the Commission will find dumping.

In the presence of different prices for different sales, many neutral observers might take an absence of dumping to be a situation in which prices have exactly the same mean and dispersion in the home market as in the export market. The rule that negative dumping will be ignored, however, means that in this situation the EEC will find 'dumping'. The reference price is calculated as a simple average of home-market prices made at a profit, while the export price is calculated by chopping off the excess over the reference price of all actual export prices. Hence, the EEC-calculated export price must be below the EEC-calculated reference price and 'dumping' will be revealed.

The legal basis for this extraordinary procedure lies in the proposition that 'negative dumping' – export sales at prices above the reference price – has no legal existence. In the EEC view, it follows that 'negative dumping prices' cannot be used to offset 'dumped' prices. It also means, however, that many exporters who would be acquitted of dumping by objective observers will be found to dump by the EEC.

Tricks with costs

Products are often sold through marketing companies associated with the manufacturer. That raises a genuine problem – the GATT recommends ex-factory prices for comparisons, but the ex-factory price of a transaction between associated companies is not necessarily the true transaction price. There are reasonable grounds for rejecting transactions between associated companies and taking instead the price of the first arms-length sale. To obtain an ex-factory price from that first arms-length sale, however, requires deduction of costs incurred between the factory and that sale. The EEC, however, does not permit allowances to be made for the overheads or advertising expenses of a related sales company in the exporter's home market. The Commission deducts such expenses on the export side of its calculation, but not in its calculation of the home-market reference price.

Suppose that a Japanese manufacturer sells an identical good at 100 to sales companies in Japan and the EEC, both of which are associated with it. Each sales company has costs per unit of 40, made up of salespeople's salaries and expenses (20), advertising (10) and overheads (10). Each sales company sells at 150 to independent retailers and has a profit of 10. Everything is identical in Japan and the EEC. The Commission, however, will discover dumping. It will deduct all expenses of the export subsidiary to arrive at a reasonable approximation of the actual ex-factory price of 100. But when it turns to the price on the Japanese market, it will deduct from the 150 price to independent retailers only 'directly related selling expenses': viz. 20 for salespeople's salaries and expenses. Thus, it will arrive at an ex-factory reference price of 130. And, comparing that reference price with the ex-factory export price of 100, it will discover a dumping margin of 30 per cent.

The effects of this methodology appear at their most bizarre when the Commission judges that there are too few sales in the home market of the exporter to take their prices as representative (as in the case of alphanumeric typewriters in Japan). It then constructs a reference price. Its objective is to obtain an ex-factory price, and it will in fact construct such a price directly. But it does not treat *that* construction as the ex-factory price. Instead, it uses it as a basis to construct the price at which sales would have been made to the first independent buyer, had there been such sales. It adds on selling expenses, advertising, overheads, profit. And then, to obtain the ex-factory price that it will use as a reference price, it deducts from this total only 'directly related selling expenses' – typically a small fraction of what it has itself added on. It will therefore finish up with an 'ex-factory price' that is larger – often much larger – than its own initial direct construction of that price. Maybe the XYZ Corporation is dumping in the EEC. But that the Commission of the European Economic Community says so is a very poor ground for that belief.

Tricks with injury

Whatever is said by EEC spokespersons, the GATT does not condemn dumping. The preamble of the GATT Anti-Dumping Code says that: '*anti-dumping practices* should not constitute an unjustifiable impediment to international trade' (emphasis added). Only after identification of *that* threat does the preamble go on to say that 'anti-dumping duties may be applied against dumping *only* if such dumping causes or threatens material injury to an established industry in the territory of a contracting party or materially retards the establishment of an industry' (emphasis added).

A recent case involving audio tapes provides an indication of the looseness of injury determination in the EEC. On 5 November 1990, provisional anti-dumping duties of up to 22.3 per cent were imposed on imports of audio-cassettes from Japan, of up to 19.4 per cent on imports from Korea, and of 2.4 per cent on imports from Hong Kong.[4] The EEC market share of cassettes imported from Japan fell from 42 to 35 per cent between 1985 and 1988 (the period covered by the investigation) – but nevertheless these imports were held by the EC to have injured EEC producers.

Part of the issue in this case is that many audio cassettes sold in the EEC under Japanese brand names are made in the EEC, legally have EEC origin, and therefore are not a legitimate target of anti-dumping action. The Commission seeks to obscure this fact (to it, no doubt, an irritating legal nicety) in its provisional determination by referring, again and again, to 'Japanese exporters', without indication of where the products of those 'exporters' are made. It says, for example, that: 'In 1985, the Japanese exporters ... achieved a 69 per cent market share ... and ... a 68 per cent share in 1988.' Even those figures hardly provide a watertight basis for an assertion that Japanese export tactics in the period injured the EC industry. The figures include, though, Japanese brands made in the EEC, which are not a target of the investigation: the market share of exports from Japan fell by seven percentage points in the relevant period.

In principle, the requirement that dumping be shown to have caused injury to domestic producers of like products provides a defence for exporters accused of dumping in the EEC. In fact, the EEC has massively eroded the ground the GATT provides.

Tricks with refunds of anti-dumping duties

Under the GATT, anti-dumping duties are supposed to be corrective, not punitive, and should in principle be refundable. The EEC, however, makes it very difficult to obtain such refunds – especially for marketing companies associated by ownership with the manufacturer of the product, a frequent structure of Japanese companies. The Commission says that in this case, 'a reimbursement will be granted if the resale price [to an independent buyer] has been increased by an amount equivalent to the margin of dumping and the amount of duty paid'.[5]

Consider an exporter to the EEC who sells through an associated sales company. His product is found to be dumped with a margin of 30 per cent, and an anti-dumping duty of 20 per cent is placed on it. The EEC gives this exporter two alternatives. He can:

(a) raise the price of his product by the 20 per cent of the anti-dumping duty and forgo refund of the duty; or he can

(b) raise the price of his product by 50 per cent (the sum of the duty and the margin) and have a chance – after a lengthy and expensive legal process – of obtaining a refund of the duty.

Either alternative is commercially damaging. EEC anti-dumping duties are punitive rather than corrective, and are very much more commercially threatening to those burdened with them than might appear from a glance at the EEC regulations.

The EEC Council of Ministers appears to recognise this. In the case of hydraulic excavators from Japan, the Council commented that '*in this particular case . . . in the light of present trade relations with Japan,* it is not in the interest of the Community to have recourse to price undertakings as an appropriate remedy for the injury resulting from dumped imports' (emphasis added).[6]

Price undertakings are a commitment by an exporter not to sell in the EEC at lower than an agreed price. The EEC makes much of the fact that many of its anti-dumping actions are settled by such undertakings, which are an alternative to anti-dumping duties. The Council's comment seems to be a clear statement that it views anti-dumping action as a political device. It implies, moreover, that the Council recognises, and is willing to use, the special punitive role that EEC regulations give to anti-dumping duties.

The provocation defence

Some observers of the events and matters reported here incline to the view that those who are hit by EEC anti-dumping action have only themselves to blame. By heavily protecting their own markets while their exports boomed, they created a situation in which retribution was inevitable. Here is Mr de Clerq, the last EEC Commissioner for External Relations, under whose regime EEC anti-dumping action flowered, writing in the *Financial Times* (21 November 1988):

> dumping is made possible only by market isolation in the exporting country, due primarily to such factors as high tariffs or non-tariff barriers and anti-competitive practices. This prevents the producers in the importing country from competing with the foreign supplier on his own ground while allowing him to attack the domestic market by sales which are often made at a loss, or are financed from the profits made from the sale of the same or related products in a protected domestic market. If anyone has doubts on the fairness of such action, he should ask the business community whether they consider it fair to compete against exporters who have accumulated supernormal profits while operating behind closed doors and then used these funds to attack the export market.

While the EEC was focusing its efforts on Japan and Korea, the argument that EEC anti-dumping policy was a reaction to closed markets elsewhere may have had some plausibility. But then the EEC turned its attention to Hong Kong. Hong Kong is a free-trading area. If EEC anti-dumping action is a reaction to protective barriers in exporting countries, Hong Kong should not be a target of EEC anti-dumping action.

Since 1988, Hong Kong has been subject to six anti-dumping actions by the EEC (concerning video tape, car telephones, small screen TVs, photograph albums, audio tape and denim cloth – even though its import into the EEC is subject to a quota!). Two more cases (concerning tungsten ore and silicon metal) involve its position as entrepot for the Peoples' Republic of China.

EEC anti-dumping policy is not a response to protection elsewhere. It is pure and simple EEC-made protectionism.

Economic costs to the EEC

The tricks and devices noted above, and others, mean that a very wide range of products can be hit by anti-dumping duties, whether or not the products are in objective terms dumped. That is a very powerful weapon in the hands of those who control the EEC anti-dumping machinery – and in the hands of EEC producers seeking protection.

The problem in assessing the costs of EEC anti-dumping policy is that the most important part of its effect appears, not in its impact on those goods that are actually subject to anti-dumping duties, but in the effect that fears of anti-dumping action will have on the prices of imported goods that are threatened with it. The EEC has established a system in which biased methods of calculation mean that any exporter to the EEC who has not raised his prices substantially above those in his home market can be found to have dumped in the EEC. It has massively eroded the grounds for defence in terms of causing injury to EEC producers. It has ensured that companies whose products are subject to anti-dumping duties will find that position commercially damaging. In these circumstances, any exporter to the EEC who thinks he might be accused of dumping has a very strong incentive to raise his EEC prices now in order to avoid anti-dumping action in the future.

The economic cost of protection by anti-dumping action is much higher than if tariffs were employed. If the price of imports rises by 30 per cent as a result of a tariff imposed by the EEC, the EEC collects revenue from the tariff. But the price of products not subject to anti-dumping duties, but open to the threat of them, will rise in reaction to that threat. If an exporter to the EEC raises his price by 30 per cent to avoid anti-dumping action by the EEC, no EEC government gets any revenue from that. Buyers of the product in the EEC are worse off –

and will be doubly worse off when the EEC producers match the price increases forced upon exporters.

The proposition that EEC producers should be protected against competition from East Asia might find wide support in the EEC. At least in part, however, that is based on the idea that East Asian producers compete unfairly – an idea encouraged by the evidence the EEC produces in the course of its frequent anti-dumping actions. But that evidence is worthless. Moreover, support for protection is not support for protection by any means. In particular, it is not support for protection based on falsehoods.

More fundamentally, EEC anti-dumping policy affects the character of the EEC itself. EEC officials and Commissioners frequently say that EEC anti-dumping action has no protectionist intent. Perhaps that is true, despite the mass of evidence to the contrary, only some of which has been given here. If it is true, though, the EEC can easily demonstrate it. The Uruguay Round gives the opportunity. The EEC can accept a new Anti-Dumping Code, designed to limit the scope for abuse of anti-dumping action in the future. In the Uruguay Round, however, the EEC has flatly rejected any amendment of the Anti-Dumping Code that threatens the use by the EEC of the tricks and devices noted above.

The cost to the multilateral trading system

So far as the GATT is concerned, the centre of the issue is Article VI of the GATT. That Article authorises (but does not require) the imposition of anti-dumping duties on dumped imports. Article VI also contains rules on the investigation of allegations of dumping and rules on the use by governments of anti-dumping duties. The rules are elaborated in the Anti-Dumping Code.

The importance of such rules is difficult to overestimate. Were GATT members allowed unrestricted access to anti-dumping action, under definitions and procedures decided by themselves, much or all of the rest of the Agreement would be deprived of effect. If each GATT member devised its own definition of dumping, and took whatever action it deemed appropriate against 'dumpers', a government could always discriminate between similar imports from different sources, merely by claiming that imports from one source were dumped.

Without the controls incorporated in Article VI and the Code, the GATT would be a multilateral agreement in form only – any contracting party could take bilateral action whenever it deemed such action to be in its interests.

Moreover, the process of bargaining in GATT that, since 1948, has continually reduced tariffs would be fatally undermined. To negotiate reciprocal reductions in levels of protection with a government that can reimpose protective barriers at a whim in the form of anti-dumping duties, cannot be a very useful activity – even for another government in the same position.

Anti-dumping policy as developed by the EEC creates a fundamental threat to the GATT. GATT authorisation of anti-dumping action poses a threat to world trade and the world trading system. As the passage quoted above at the start of the section on injury clearly says, Article VI of the GATT is intended to control that threat by controlling anti-dumping action. The EEC has emasculated those controls. That places the survival of the GATT as an effective body of international law in jeopardy. It is potentially as damaging as the EEC-produced impasse over agriculture.

EEC Interests

In trade policy, the EEC pursues, as it should, its own self-interest. The version of its self-interest that it pursues, however, is of dubious validity. To prop up inefficient EEC producers, at great expense to other EEC residents, is not a view of EEC economic interests that is universally held, even leaving aside effects on other countries and on the world trading system as a whole. Moreover, the propping-up is often achieved by corrupt means – by illusion and manipulation.

The EEC, however, is the largest trading entity in the world. It has an interest in the character of the world trading system, and its actions affect that system. Any sensible interpretation of EEC self-interest must take account of those facts. Current EEC trade policy does not take account of them.

Those who are urging a federal future for the EEC often do so on the basis that a federal EEC will have more influence in the world at large. That might be true. But those who support the federalist position seem to assume as a matter of course that greater EEC influence will make the world a better place. The performance of the EEC in trade policy, which the Treaty of Rome places in the hands of the EEC institutions, does not bear out that assumption. That performance suggests the possibility that a federal EEC would create an immobile and introverted lump in world affairs, whose primary effect would be to neuter the better instincts of individual member states and to give them more power to pursue their worst instincts. EEC trade policy has not improved the world trading system. A federal Europe that behaved in a similar manner on a wider stage would not improve the world.

The EEC has the power to influence the world trading system for better or for worse. Before EEC competence is extended, it should demonstrate that it can use that power for useful purposes. If it could bring itself to do that, both the EEC and the world would be the better for it.

Notes

1 The notion that the CAP is a foundation-stone of the EEC presumably is based on the incorporation in the Treaty of Rome of Title 11 ('Agriculture'). Title 11 certainly makes a common policy towards agriculture a foundation-stone of the EEC. Whether it justifies the present CAP, however, is dubious. Article 39(1)(e), for example, requires a policy that 'ensure[s] that supplies reach consumers at reasonable prices'. Moreover, the focus of Article 39 is on assistance to agricultural labour, whereas the CAP primarily increases returns to land (see Chapter 5).

2 The following passage was written before the negotiation was completed. The spirit of the observations it contains however, continues to apply to the actual Association Agreements.

3 Not that the US ideas did not have European admirers. The *Economist*, commenting on proposals made by the US in 1942, said: 'Let there be no mistake about it. The policy put forward by the American Administration is revolutionary. It is a genuinely new conception of world order. It is an inspiring attempt to restate democracy in terms of the twentieth century situation, and to extend its meaning in the economic and social sphere.' Quoted in Gardner, 1956, p.1.

4 Official Journal of the European Communities, L313/5 of 13 November 1990.

5 Ball Bearings originating in Singapore (refunds) (Official Journal of the European Communities, L148, 1988)

6 Official Journal of the European Communities, L176/4, 6 July 1985.

References

Gardner, R. N. (1956) *Sterling-Dollar Diplomacy*, Oxford University Press

Hindley, B (1988) 'Dumping and the Far East trade of the European Community', *The World Economy* (December)

Hirsch, Seev (1988) 'Antidumping actions in Brussels and East-West trade', *The World Economy* (December)

Johnson, H. G. (1971) 'Optimal trade intervention in the presence of domestic distortions' in Johnson (ed.), *Aspects of the Theory of Tariffs* (London: Allen and Unwin)

Krugman, P. (1982) 'The macroeconomics of protection with a floating exchange rate', *Carnegie-Rochester Conference Series on Public* 16

Mundell, R. (1961) "Flexible exchange rates and employment policy" *Canadian Journal of Economics and Political Science* (November)

7 *Martin Holmes*

Eastern Europe and the EEC

Introduction

The momentous revolutionary events of 1989 took the twelve EEC countries – and much of the rest of the world – by surprise. Gorbachev's perestroika was not anticipated to sanction an end to Soviet imperial dominion over the Warsaw Pact countries where change was expected to be peripheral, on the model of gradual reform as in Kadar's Hungary. Even those people with a special interest in – and sympathy towards – the peoples of Eastern Europe, including this author, were not predicting a sudden collapse of communism. I remember attending, in December 1988, a four-hour seminar at Warsaw University's Economics Department on 'Privatising the Polish economy'. Never had a topic seemed so academic – yet so practically imperative to hauling Poland's economy into the modern age. The chairman of our seminar, a dynamic Solidarity economist, was Professor Leszek Balcerowicz who conducted our discussion at a brisk pace. None of us around the conference table suspected, let alone knew, that within twelve months the Communist regimes in Poland and elsewhere in Eastern Europe would be swept away. In their place democracy would replace dictatorship and market economies would start to emerge, albeit at a different pace in each country. Similarly on a short visit to Ceausescu's Romania in December 1989 it was entirely by chance, not expectation, that I found myself in Timisoara observing the events which began the Romanian revolution.[1]

But while many people rejoiced at the fall of European communism, the reaction of the EEC was muted and lukewarm. The dramatic events in the East seemed to presage the vision of a wider Europe of independent democratic sovereign states 'from the Atlantic to the Urals' in de Gaulle's memorable phrase. Similarly, as Mrs Thatcher had argued in her 1988 Bruges speech, 'Europe' comprised the whole continent in which 'Prague, Warsaw and Budapest were great European cities'. By contrast, while publicly applauding the newly-won freedom, the EEC privately felt, in French foreign minister Roland Dumas' words, less 'comfortable'.

Taken by surprise by the speed of change in the East, the EEC feared the ending of the comfortable world in which the division of Europe was the front line in the ideological and military cold war and where the twain of East and West would never meet. This negative attitude was clearly apparent during the August 1991 coup by hardline communists in the Soviet Union. President Mitterrand, in a television broadcast, seemed to accept that the Gorbachev era was over by giving an equivocal response to the new regime. Other EEC leaders reacted with a paralysed caution of 'wait and see'.

While Mrs Thatcher urged immediate support for Boris Yeltsin, the Socialist-dominated European Parliament, whose members had insulted Yeltsin on his visit there in April, were still expressing doubts even after the coup's failure. Glyn Ford, the Labour group leader, claimed that Yeltsin 'often appears to be an extreme nationalist . . . [he] said that Russians should not shoot Russians. I hope that he's not in favour of Russians shooting Ukrainians, or Ukrainians shooting Russians, or anybody shooting anybody.'[2] Such a response to Mr Yeltsin's triumph reflected the EEC unease at the changing nature of European politics which challenged the basis of the exclusivity of a community of twelve.

The response from the EEC was entirely predictable. The Six had come together in 1957 when the shadows of Hitler and Stalin were still cast across the Continent. Moreover, the military standoff of NATO and the Warsaw Pact was now replicated by an economic standoff of COMECON and the EEC. Political co-operation across the Iron Curtain was non-existent; economic and trading links were negligible. Writing as late as 1985, Prof. Hine in his study of EEC trade policy noted that:

> The future prospects for EEC-COMECON trade are uncertain, and a number of factors suggest that the growth of trade in the 1980s will be less rapid than in the past. These factors include the slowdown in economic growth in both East and West, increased political tension, growing EEC protectionism in areas in which COMECON countries have an export interest (e.g. agriculture, textiles and steel), EEC tariff preferences for rival developing country sup-

pliers, and the need for East European countries to increase their exports to the USSR in order to meet the increased cost of their oil supplies.[3]

Nor was the trading relationship with the other two non-Warsaw-Pact non-COMECON countries much better. With Albania, links of any kind were discouraged by Enver Hoxha's Stalinist regime; with Yugoslavia, the EEC pursued a policy of strictly managed trade and protectionist devices which made a mockery of the 1970 Yugoslav-EEC Agreement.[4] Subsequent agreements, negotiated by the EEC-Yugoslavia Joint Committee, regulated virtually every aspect of trade, so that Yugoslavia was guaranteed a place on the list of beneficiaries of the EEC Generalised Scheme of Preference (GSP). This scheme theoretically gives Yugoslavia freedom from customs duties for industrial products and partial exemption for certain processed farm products. But in reality, a vast network of tariff and other barriers exists against Yugoslav products, of all kinds.

First, there is the problem of agricultural protectionism arising from the Common Agricultural Policy (CAP). Yugoslavia's agricultural exports are almost entirely subject to the rules of the CAP, excluding them from its scheme of generalised preferences. The variability and stagnation of Yugoslav exports to the Community in the first few years of the Co-operation Agreement was mainly due to the full implementation of the CAP on Yugoslav agricultural exports. Thus, in 1985, food and drink accounted for 9.1 per cent of total Yugoslav exports. By 1987, this figure had fallen to 8.1 per cent. Other aspects of protectionism further reduce trade. The structure of the EEC common tariff still uses tariff escalation, which acts as a considerable barrier to price competitiveness. This explains, for example, why Yugoslavia exports more live animals than meat products to the EEC.

Second, Yugoslavia is accused of dumping, in many different cases out of proportion to its share of the EEC market. In fact, anti-dumping measures affect 60 per cent of Yugoslavia's exports to the EEC, including textiles and clothes, farm products, and all 'sensitive' manufactured goods. Within the EEC it is the producers who, unable to compete with Yugoslav goods at current market conditions, file complaints initiating the anti-dumping investigations. As with all protectionism, the winner is the producer – while the losers are both the Yugoslav exporters and the EEC consumers who have to pay the subsequent higher prices.

Twenty years after the signing of the 1970 Yugoslav-EEC Agreement, therefore, the primary EEC concern was to limit, rather than to expand, trade. Given that Yugoslavia was a non-aligned country which wished to expand contacts with the EEC, the response from Brussels did not augur well for the other Eastern European nations with the exception of East Germany after the 1989 revolutions. Not surprisingly, the EEC response to the war in Yugoslavia was to impose economic sanctions indiscriminately on victims and aggressor alike.

The EEC response: humanitarian

The immediate EEC response to the collapse of communism during the winter of 1989-90 was to provide humanitarian aid. In this endeavour the EEC, along with the United States and international agencies, made a necessary and generous contribution. Food aid alone totalled £140 million by December 1990, principally to Poland and the Soviet Union. Food stocks in Berlin – set aside for a cold war-style blockade – were rushed to Moscow in the winter of 1990-1. Similarly, after the fall of the Stalinist regime in Albania between March and June 1991, the EEC dispatched medicines and food, primarily cereals, from the CAP's unsold stockpiles. In September the EEC Commission even paid $5.9 million to buy 45,000 tons of Hungarian wheat to offset Albanian food shortages. This record was somewhat tarnished, however, by the unsympathetic treatment of Albanian refugees by the Italian authorities. 2,500 refugees, who were told they were being flown to Rome, were instead flown back to Albania. According to one Italian policeman, when the Albanians recognised their own coastlines there were cries of anger but no violence.[5]

Individual countries, notably Germany, have also provided additional humanitarian assistance to Eastern Europe, though such generosity may not be totally unrelated to the 1990 fears generated by reunification.[6] For example, Germany has contributed up to half of the total humanitarian aid to the Soviet Union.

The EEC response: political

The EEC's political response to the new democracies in central and Eastern Europe has been negative and, when explained, wholly unconvincing. Instead of embracing the countries of Eastern Europe by offering immediate EEC membership – or membership within a few years – Brussels has closed the door and prevaricated with talk of distant liaisons and association agreements. The EEC has clung to the cold war model of a divided Europe, despite the dissolution of the Warsaw Pact and the statesmanlike evolution of NATO to the changed circumstances. Nor can public pressure explain or excuse EEC reluctance to expand its membership; EEC citizens have reacted favourably to the idea of new members, with for example 63 per cent of British respondents advocating admission of the Eastern European countries.[7]

The EEC's reluctance is not difficult to explain. As Russell Lewis has pointed out, administrative convenience is one reason. The EEC finds it difficult enough with eleven languages, let alone double this number; Jacques Delors once stated that: 'I can manage twelve countries but not fifteen or twenty-four.'[8] The sheer administrative upheaval of disrupting the 'Twelve' daunts the Brussels bureaucracy. More significant is the EEC's determination to complete the plans hatched before the 1989 Eastern European revolutions. The 1992 Single Market programme, the moves to monetary union with a Single Currency, and the political integration of existing nation-states into a centralised 'federal' union are all based on the exclusivity of the Twelve. Moreover, they are based on notions of centralisation to limit national sovereignty, which the Eastern democracies find repugnant. Admission of the Eastern Europeans would dilute the federalists' dreams. As Mrs Thatcher pointed out at Aspen, Colorado, in August 1990:

'I propose that the Community should declare unequivocally that it is ready to accept all the countries of Eastern Europe as members if they want to join, and when democracy has taken root and their economies are capable of sustaining membership. We can't say in one breath that they are part of Europe, and in the next our European Community Club is so exclusive that we won't admit them . . . But if instead we set off down the path of giving more and more powers to highly centralised institutions, which are not democratically accountable, then we should be making it harder for the Eastern Europeans to join. They have not thrown off central command and control in their own countries only to find them reincarnated in the European Community.'[9]

Similarly in June 1991 Mrs Thatcher noted that the advocates of a federal Europe were actively placing obstacles in the way of wider membership: 'they do not want ancient European nations like Poland and Hungary influencing the development of common European institutions because their experience of communism has made them suspicious of centralised bureaucracy and attentive to the claims of national sovereignty.'[10]

Even after the failure of the hardline coup in the Soviet Union, the

EEC was still reluctant to support independence for the Baltic republics until it became an inevitability. On 23 August Jacques Delors told the European Parliament that 'romantic nationalism' was horribly expensive, adding that: 'We cannot unite the states of Western Europe and at the same time encourage the breakaway of Soviet republics.'[11]

Not surprisingly, therefore, attempts by Eastern European countries to join the EEC – as part of a wider Europe or a common European home – have been rebutted. Indeed, it is suspicious that the EEC has dragged its feet over the applications of Turkey, Austria, Sweden (and possibly other EFTA countries) in an attempt to delay still further the applications from the East. The 1991 Inter-Governmental Conferences' negotiations over economic and political union have also provided a heroic pretext to put expanded membership – and a different European political structure – on the back burner. The consequences of such a policy, as the Bruges Group secretary pointed out in Warsaw, are damaging for countries such as Poland:

> the new European Union would have exclusive control over foreign, defence, social, industrial, educational, cultural and environmental policy. The result would be a federal Europe, with nation-states reduced to the status of provinces within a bureaucratic, sclerotic and all-powerful western European superstate.
>
> In order to achieve this goal, the governments of western Europe do not support the membership of any other countries until the process is completed. In fact, they will not even discuss new applications until 1995 – at least two years after the new Treaty of Union is ratified and implemented. This means that if Polish membership of the Community is difficult today, it will be impossible after 1 January 1993. In the meantime, western governments will seek to pacify central and eastern European countries with promises of Association Agreements, and membership of countless European organisations on the fringes of real power.[12]

Like Poland, Czechoslovakia has also found the current EEC policy unhelpful. On a visit to Prague in 1991 French president Francois Mitterrand suggested that the EC remain the same, with a loose confederation of nations lying beyond its boundaries. When M. Mitterrand aired his confederation concept Czechoslovak president Vaclav Havel said firmly that his country's long-term aim was to join the Community. Significantly supporting Mrs Thatcher's position President Havel has called for Europe to be 'a friendly community of independent nations and sovereign states . . . not divided into blocs and pacts. We have awakened and we must awake those in Europe who have slept through our awakening.'[13] Although he did not name names or blocs, there is no mistaking President Havel's criticism of the EEC's stance.

Along with the Poles and Czechs, the Hungarians have also encountered a frosty reception from the EEC with the prospect of discussions on an association agreement the only option. But Romania and Bulgaria, who have only requested association agreements, have been informed that this cannot be considered until 'talks with Poland, Czechoslovakia and Hungary have been finalised'[14] This blatant delaying tactic does not augur well for co-operation in the wider democratic Europe. Indeed a Europe of independent sovereign states co-operating together for mutual benefit is not on the EEC's agenda and nor is it likely to be following Mrs Thatcher's removal from power.

The EEC response: economic

The primary economic policy response to the events of 1989 has been to preserve the protectionist customs union nature of EEC trade policy and to resist any moves to free trade. 'Managed trade' on a mercantilist model has always been the EEC's external policy, and the Brussels Commission has no intention of adopting a Cobdenite trade policy to Eastern Europe (or anywhere else for that matter). This policy, however, is mitigated by the provision of 'aid' and 'development funds' in exactly the same way as provided by the EEC to Third World countries. To alleviate the trade losses to third countries incurred as a result of, for example, the protectionist stance of the CAP, the EEC provides 'compensation' through grants and loans.[15]

Before examining the effects of EEC trade policy on the Eastern European countries it is worthwhile to concentrate briefly on the developmental assistance now available to them not least because of the extensive media attention it has received. Although individual EEC countries have provided technical and financial assistance to them to assist their transformation into market economies, the bulk of EEC aid is channelled through the European Bank for Reconstruction and Development (EBRD).

The brainchild of President Mitterrand, the EBRD is financed by contributions from the United States, Japan and Western Europe and is directed by Jacques Attali. A former professor of economics and French Socialist Party member, Attali was economic adviser to Mitterrand and architect of the ill-fated nationalisation policies of 1981-4 from which the French economy was rescued by loans from the IMF and Saudi Arabia. Attali has little time for the free market, preferring, in the French mercantilist tradition of Colbert, centralised co-ordination between private and public sectors. He has thus not only championed formal nationalisation, but has advocated the subsidised 'European' Airbus and the promotion of 'European' high-definition television. On a visit to Prague in 1991 Attali surprised his Czech hosts by praising the Communist Party's stewardship of the city between 1948 and 1989. According to Attali, the free market took hundreds of years to emerge in Western Europe and may take as long in the East. In short, Attali is not a man to inspire confidence as a facilitator of free- market reform in Eastern Europe.

So far the EBRD's performance has only confirmed the doubts of those, such as William Niskanen, the Cato Institute's Washington chairman, who argued that: 'I think the last thing these eastern European countries need is money that will defer the most important decisions.'[16] For example, Jessica Douglas Home complained that a request for funds for a joint venture in Romania was rejected because they did not conform to the Romanian government's plan! Similarly this author, whose Polish partner approached the EBRD with a joint venture business proposal in Gdansk, was informed that '[the EBRD] . . . hope to address the needs of this segment of the economy on a more global level by creating and collaborating with financial intermediaries and business advisories . . .'.[17] In short, M. Attali's EBRD may do more harm than good to the process of building markets, while providing a convenient human face to disguise the EEC's protectionist trade policy.

Although Article 110 of the Treaty of Rome committed the EEC to 'contribute to the harmonious development of world trade, the gradual removal of obstacles to international trade, and the dismantling of customs barriers', the reality since 1957 has been very different. The EEC has striven to lower internal barriers (1992 etc.), but to increase external barriers, both tariff and non-tariff. The EEC's favourite devices are 'voluntary' export agreements, quotas, anti-dumping regulations and quantitative controls. The CAP is arguably the world's most protectionist organisation which, notwithstanding Japanese rice import restrictions, was responsible for the collapse of the Uruguay Round of GATT in December 1990. In April 1991 an IMF survey concluded that 'the trade wall around the EEC has risen and will rise even higher in the years ahead'. In the same month the GATT review of EEC trade policy concluded that 'it is time that the EEC matched its internal integration with a parallel lifting of its external barriers and closer adherence to the fundamental principles underlying the multilateral trading system'.

Commenting on the GATT report, the *Financial Times* editorial noted that:

Yesterday's report on European Community trade policy by the General Agreement on Tariffs and Trade is refreshingly robust. Though few will be surprised by the thrust of the report's criticisms of the EC, it can only be healthy for the trading system that they should be brought into the open . . . The EC does, as the Gatt complains, suffer from a tendency to respond to particular trade problems with targeted bilateral solutions – abuse of its anti-dumping rules, for example, or recourse to voluntary restraint arrangements. It does also operate a complex web of discriminatory preferential arrangements with the European Free Trade Association, Mediterranean countries and developing nations.

The EC's reply that it is still a large importer, even of the most heavily restricted products such as farm goods, textiles, steel and cars, is lame. Nor is it any excuse to defend one's own barriers on the grounds that others have restrictions too.

The true message underlying the report is that there is a culture of protectionism at work in the EC. Whatever the record on Fortress Europe until now, there is a danger that this culture will come to dominate as the Uruguay Round grows more difficult. Already, there are unpleasant signs of protection gaining ground. After a period of apparent restraint, the Commission's traditional sleight of hand is reappearing in calculating dumping margins on video cassettes and tapes. The number of dumping cases in the pipeline has swollen, while the granting of such procedural forms of protection remains too obscure in both its underlying rationale and its results.

To its shame the EC has also baulked at opening up its borders to farm products, textiles and steel from the emerging market economies of Eastern Europe. There could scarcely be a better way of undermining the political reforms so earnestly sought by the West for more than four decades.[18]

Given the fundamentally protectionist ideology of the EEC, it is not surprising that the new democracies of Eastern Europe have not been offered free trade. In particular, the areas where Eastern Europe already enjoys a comparative advantage – agriculture, textiles and steel – are subject to the greatest barriers. In Hungary, for example, 70 per cent of the land is suitable for agriculture, 50 per cent of it arable, yet the CAP blocks Hungarian exports. Bulgaria has received EEC 'development aid' of £200 million, but its wine exports are severely circumscribed by the CAP. A similar situation has long existed in Yugoslavia. The damage inflicted by EEC protectionism on the Yugoslav economy is, albeit in part, responsible for the collapse of civil order in areas of the country. Nor does the EEC's protectionist policy benefit the twelve member states, as it both denies consumer choice and generates political instability. As *The European* rightly argued:

> Urgent steps must be taken to bring down the trade barriers which restrict imports from eastern Europe to the more prosperous west . . .
>
> Western governments have been ready to give financial aid to eastern Europe but less enthusiastic to open their markets to competition. Europe's leaders must show a wider vision than this. There is little purpose in ordering these former communist states to become market economies if they are denied access to markets. Protectionism remains formidably strong in western Europe. It is an indictment of many companies' commercial inadequacy that they are frightened of competition from the outmoded businesses of eastern Europe. Only free and fair trade will enable all Europe to prosper. A continent that remains divided between the rich west and the poor east would stoke up resentment and bitterness. The Iron Curtain must not be replaced by the trade wall.[19]

The position of Poland exemplifies the nature of EEC trade policy. Of all the countries in Eastern Europe, Poland has made the greatest strides towards transforming its economy to market disciplines. Inflation has been tamed, market pricing has eliminated queues, overseas investment has been sought, and privatisation is on the agenda. Polish economic reform, like that in Eastern Europe, has been conducted to the background noises of encouragement from the West in general and the EEC in particular. But just how far has EEC policy helped Poland? On the credit side, emergency food aid was provided in winter 1989-90 and a sympathetic approach to Poland's external debt is official policy. But such assistance is essentially related to the current period of transforming the command socialist model to a private enterprise one. The longer-term relationship between the EEC and a Polish market economy has not been considered. The evidence for this lies in the EEC-Polish trade agreement concluded with the Solidarity government in December 1989.

Like other similar agreements with the former communist states, the agreement is designed for managed trade on a mercantilist model, not free trade. In this respect it is similar to the agreement originally signed in 1970 between the EEC and Yugoslavia which effectively denies the Yugoslavs access to the EEC market for the products which they most wish to export, and for which EEC consumers have the greatest demand. The EEC-Polish agreement in Articles 1 and 2 makes a promising start, declaring that: 'The two Parties undertake to facilitate and promote trade and economic cooperation with each other. The Contracting Parties reaffirm their commitment to afford each other most-favoured nation treatment in accordance with the General Agreement on Tariffs and Trade (GATT) and the Protocol for the accession of Poland thereto.'

But Articles 3 and 4 introduce the sort of protectionist exceptions for which the EEC is notorious worldwide – steel, textiles and agriculture:

> This Agreement shall apply to trade in all products originating in the Community or in Poland with the exception of the products covered by the Treaty establishing the European Coal and Steel Community.
>
> This Agreement shall not affect the provisions of the existing Agreements concerning trade in textile products between the Community and Poland, nor of any agreements subsequently concluded in the same field.
>
> This Agreement shall not affect specific agreements or arrangements covering agricultural products in force between the Contracting Parties, or any successor agreements or arrangements.[20]

Already the Poles (and EEC consumers) are the losers, and EEC producers the protected winners. However, even more specific and restrictive protectionist measures are subsequently documented affecting Polish exports to all, or some, EEC countries. Quantitative restrictions, duties, and levies are applied to:

Horses for slaughter.
Ducks, plucked and drawn, known as '63 per cent ducks'.
Geese, plucked and drawn, known as '75 per cent geese'.
Boned or boneless cuts of geese, excluding offals.
Unboned breasts and cuts of breasts of geese.
Unboned legs and cuts of legs of geese.
Strawberries, preserved by freezing, not containing added sugar.
Sausages, dry or for spreading, cooked, other than liver sausage.
Other preparations of meat and offal of domestic swine, with any fats, containing 80 per cent or more of meat other than ham, loins, collars, shoulders or bovine meat.
Cabbage lettuce, from 1 January to 15 June and from 15 November to 31 December.

Beans (of the species Phaseolus), from 1 to 30 June.
Flour and meal for human consumption.
Potatoes prepared or preserved other than by vinegar or acetic acid.
Butylxylol for the manufacture of musc, xylene and divinylbenzol.
Chloromethane, excluding ethylene dibromide, excluding isobutylic alcohol.
4-Aminosalicylic acid and its salts and esters.
Leather, other than spectacle cases.
Webs of cellulose fibres.
Strawpaper.
Paper board, excluding press board (press-span).
Jars, pots and similar containers of blown or pressed glass, excluding feeding-bottles for infants and aquariums.
Mattresses, other than of rubber, quilts, and eiderdowns.
Cushions, other than of expanded rubber.

The agreement, in short, has very little to do with freer trade, let alone genuinely free trade.[21]

At the moment, when transforming the Polish economy to the market is the priority, talk of free trade may sound esoteric. But if Poland's transformation occurs sooner rather than later, then access to over 320 million EEC customers will move up the economic and political agenda. The EEC's policy of protectionist managed trade will frustrate this process unless serious attention is given to genuine trade liberalisation involving the discarding of the policies which now threaten to create 'Fortress Europe'. More than that, the current fear is that EEC trade agreements similar to that with Poland will actually hinder the process of market-oriented reform by restricting export markets and denying foreign exchange.

Although negotiations between the EEC and Poland to replace the 1989 Agreement have continued throughout 1991, there is no sign that the EEC will adopt a free-trade position especially on the 'sensitive' issues of agriculture, textiles and steel. As the Polish trade negotiator Mr Olechowski put it in March 1991, 'our markets are open – now we want you to open yours.' President Walesa has been even more critical of EEC trade policy, observing that:

> We allow imports of all goods but the West is not buying ours. Why are we being punished? We could end up like Romania which has nothing but shortages. If we don't find a common language my farmers won't allow food from

the West. But this is not what should be happening. We've achieved so much so subtly. We've handed Europe victory on a plate, and the opportunity to link all Europe up on a healthy basis. Yet just look at what Europe is doing. It does not want to get involved . . . it hums and haws. Generations have fought for this great chance. Well, now we have it. The question is, will we screw it up? Everything ought to be possible – entry into NATO, into the European Community, everything. But what are we doing? Just waiting for the next earthquake. It's amazing. Incredible.[22]

Even on the assumption of some long-term liberalisation of EEC trade policy towards Eastern Europe, it is likely that the policy of managed trade will hinder the market transformation process, thereby preventing the Eastern Europeans from achieving full – or even partial – prosperity. As one senior GATT negotiator has shrewdly noted, the EEC's 1992 project has 'top billing' over both a successful conclusion to the Uruguay Round and also reconstruction in Eastern Europe.[23]

It was no surprise, therefore, when eight months of trade talks between the EEC and Eastern European countries broke down in September 1991. Although the ostensible cause of the breakdown was a French objection to a miniscule increase of 550 metric tonnes a year of beef imports, it was always likely that the political will was lacking to achieve any trade liberalisation. Portugal had pressed for continued textile protectionism and Germany had agonised over steel and coal imports. Without a comprehensive reform, or effective dismantling of the CAP, which the EEC would not permit, any agreement with Eastern European countries would lack credibility. Managed trade, not free trade, was the EEC's offer, but even modest concessions within the managed trade framework proved too much for many, but not all, member states. The Danish Foreign Minister, Utte Ellemann-Jensen, castigated his colleagues:'this is a disgrace . . . there seems to be a small faction here that is living on another planet.'[24] Alas, it appeared that the small faction was that which favoured freer trade, and the EEC majority view remained essentially protectionist.

Conclusions

In many ways the prospects for Eastern Europe are good, especially following the collapse of communism in the Soviet Union. The transition to democracy is completed in most, but not all, countries. The hard road to the market has been embarked upon in each country, albeit at a faster and more successful pace in some countries than in others.

The peoples of Eastern Europe are rejoining the mainstream of European political, cultural and economic life from which they were cut off first by fascism and then by communism. Those westerners who travel regularly to Eastern Europe, including this author, cannot but admire the ingenuity, resourcefulness and sheer survivability of the people. Their democratic stability is in our interests, and their economic prosperity is to our advantage as a new market for western products. The attitude of the EEC is not the only pitfall the Eastern European countries face – religious or ethnic strife may be just as ghastly there as it is in Ulster or the Basque country. But the EEC's current policy, both political and economic, hinders rather than helps the Eastern Europeans. We in the EEC should heed Mrs Thatcher's grim warning:'a new wall – a wealth wall – has arisen in Europe to replace the Berlin Wall. And the instability of Eastern Europe may be prolonged and aggravated as a result.'[25]

Notes

1 For an account of my observations see 'Timisoara and the demise of Stalinism', *Sydney Papers*, Vol. 2 No. 1, Winter 1990, Sydney Institute publications, Australia.
2 *The Times*, 23 August 1991.
3 R. C. Hine, *The Political Economy of European Trade*, Harvester Wheatsheaf, 1985, pp. 250-51.
4 For a full account see M. Holmes, *Yugoslavia and the EEC*, Bruges Group Publications, 1990.
5 *The Times*, 19 August 1991.
6 In the view of this author such fears were always misplaced. Any 'threat' to European freedom comes not from any single country, including Germany, but from an over-centralised, inward-looking bureaucratic superstate based on the EEC Commission in Brussels.
7 See Audience Selection poll reported in *Contemporary Record*, April 1990.
8 Russell Lewis, *Master Eurocrat – the making of Jacques Delors*, Bruges Group Publications, 1991.
9 Speech at Aspen, Colorado, 5 August 1990.
10 Speech at Chicago, 17 June 1991.
11 *The Times*, 24 August 1991.
12 Patrick Robertson, speech in Warsaw, 23 January 1991.
13 President Havel's speech was delivered to the Polish Parliament, 21 January 1990.
14 Reported in *The European*, 26 July 1991.

15 It must be pointed out, however, that in 1989-90 the CAP cost Third World countries £2 billion in lost exports, while EEC 'aid' totalled £1 billion.
16 Quoted in *Wall Street Journal Europe*, Eastern Europe survey, 1 October 1990.
17 Letter from EBRD, 26 April 1991.
18 *Financial Times*, 17 April 1991.
19 *The European*, 26 January 1991.
20 EEC-Polish Trade Agreement, December 1989.
21 *Ibid.*
22 Quoted in the *Wall Street Journal Europe*, 24 April 1991.
23 See Alan Oxley, *The Challenge of Free Trade*, Harvester Wheatsheaf, 1990, p. 91.
24 *New York Times*, 1 September 1991.
25 Speech in Chicago, 17 June 1991.

PART III

UNIFICATION: EVOLUTION OR STANDARDISATION?

8 *Alan Walters*

Britain and the Exchange Rate Mechanism

Britain's formal entry into the ERM followed a long engagement. Informally, however, she had been shacking up with the ERM since February 1987. Indeed, for the year to March 1988, sterling was more stable than the French franc with respect to the Deutschmark priority. The British mistress or fiancé was more faithful than the French wife. The commitment in October 1990 simply put an official seal on the three-and-half-year affair. The idea was that fitful and flighty Britain would be able to borrow the legendary stability of the German economy and currency, so ably managed by the Bundesbank. One of the warnings that I have frequently given (perhaps too frequently as with the boy who cried wolf) is that one would be unwise to rely on the record of stability of Germany in the future. I recalled that in the interwar years everyone thought that sterling was the most stable currency, and in the 1950s and early 1960s an inflating US dollar was quite unthinkable. Can we be so sure that Germany will not slip off the path of monetary virtue?

Over 1991-92 the great Deutschemark has had its own troubles. The stable and sure 'anchor' (as Mr Samuel Brittan calls it) has been dragging rather alarmingly, pulled by the Eastern *länder*, devaluing against the dollar, sinking near the bottom of its band and showing every sign of the British disease. A passing phase? The Europhiles certainly hope so. But it has made life much easier for Britain during this first year of formal entry. It is ironic that the erosion of the very reason for ERM membership – German stability – has eased Britain's entry.

Meanwhile, we have seen the absurdity of the interest rate structure of the ERM countries and their dependencies distorted upwards by the persistent appreciation of the ERM's most inflationary currency, the peseta (although the lira runs a close second). Still the peseta rules –

and incidentally verifies what has been called the 'Walters critique' as Spain inflates at 6.5 per cent. Soon, no doubt, we shall see a combined devaluation of the peseta and a commitment to the 2.25 per cent band.

What of Britain? Certainly the period 1987-91 has been a Götterdämmerung – the twilight of the Thatcher years. From 1987, when she allowed Lawson to shadow the mark, Mrs Thatcher conceded much of macroeconomic policy to the Europhiles. First, the pegging of the pound at Dm 3, by promoting interest rates as low as 7.5 per cent in 1988, generated the 10 per cent inflation of 1990-91. Then interest rates at 14-15 per cent brought down inflation down from its 1990-91 levels to less than 4 per cent in 1991. A diet of castor oil followed by kaopectate may well demonstrate respectively the efficacy of laxative and bung, but the patient is surely better off if he abstains from both.

Commentators in the *Financial Times* (Martin Wolf, 4 October 1991) and the *Economist* (5 and 11 October 1991) are, apparently, not so sure. For example, in February I (together with five others comprising the 'Liverpool Six') commented that monetary policy, duly constrained by the ERM commitment, was too tight. Yet, says Wolf, interest rates came down by 3 per cent over the next three months. But Mr Wolf and the *Economist* surely know that it is monetary growth and *real* interest rates, not nominal rates, that are indicators of monetary tightness. On both these criteria policy has tightened, not eased, since formal entry in October 1990. In October 1991 with base rate at 10.5 per cent, we had an expected inflation rate of less than 4 per cent, and similarly today in mid-1992: so real interest rates are 6.5 to 7.0 per cent. If indeed if we take wage costs per unit of output as our measure of inflation, which according to the *Economist* had ceased rising over 1991, this implies real interest rates of over 10 per cent – rather high by any criteria. The Liverpool Six thought that the tight monetary policy to January 1991 would deepen the slump. It is not obvious that we were wrong. The *Economist*, however, trumpeted 'Rejoice.' 'Britain's first year in the (ERM) has been a great success. Really.' And its final clincher is the 'sharp narrowing of bond yields' against Germany during the year. This is thinly disguised *Schadenfreude*.

One of my continuing arguments against all pegged systems and the ERM in particular is that it provides perverse monetary policies. The *Economist* said that 'as a piece of economic theory, this view [Walters' critique] cannot be faulted', and the writer conceded that Spain has been a worked example of the critique. (The *Economist*, however, printed my picture with 'proved wrong', and Lawson's with 'proved right' – a manifestation of editorial consistency perhaps?) Both Wolf and the *Economist* contrasted my saying that in 1987-89 the ERM would induce too lax a policy with my affirmation in late 1990 to 1991 that it induced too tight a policy. But this is the essence of my critique. The exchange rate peg twists interest rates and capital flows to exacerbate inflation or deflation, boom and slump.

In my *Independent* article of 13 July 1988, I forecast a 'roller coaster' of a ride on the ERM. We have not been disappointed: the complete ride of the roller coaster lasted from February 1987 to the last half of 1991, just about the 4 to 5 years that is the average period of the trade cycle. A coincidence? Perhaps – although I would beware of too many coincidences. And there has been the special factor of Germany deviating from the path of monetary virtue, and proving to be much more lenient in disciplining Britain's efforts to find again that stern path of monetary rectitude. Inflation has come down to less than 4 per cent (indeed as I forecast in the summer of 1990), true. But we are in deep and persistent recession, with unemployment rising to some 3 million. And although many a swallow of recovery has been sighted in the autumnal and winter skies, I am sure that output will remain well below capacity and unemployment well above the tolerable level for many months to come.

We are assured by the *cognoscenti* in the *Economist* that now we are in the ERM interest rates, inflation and unemployment will be kept low. Stability, we are told, will be a natural consequence of lashing sterling to the Mark mast. Alas, I do not think so. And somewhat late in the day on June 22 1992 Martin Wolf in the *Financial Times* produced a graph entitled 'The UK economy's roller-coaster ride' pointing out that 'the macroeconomic instability of the last five years has been considerable. Why should we not repeat the errors of 1987 all over again – with the same exchange rate, but at a somewhat lower level of employment and activity? I see no reason to suppose that we shall not get on the roller coaster for another ride. We may, of course, fall off – perhaps with a few companions. But I suspect the politicians will strap us all firmly in place, and no whimpering. The ride is likely to start again in 1993 or perhaps 1994 when a boom will begin to develop – like that of 1987-8 – as a consequence of monetary expansion fuelled in part by capital imports and in part, domestically, by lower interest rates to contain the capital inflow. By 1995-6 inflation will again be pressing, and policy will be switched. But it will take at least two years to bring it under control – which takes us to 1997-8, when inflation will fall again rather suddenly to below 4 per cent. And so the cycle is complete and we shall be back again to the conditions of the autumnal months of 1991 – recession redux.

Some people apparently find roller coasters thrilling, but I suspect that most of us find them merely sick-making. We could, of course, get off. We could walk away and leave this curious continental masochism to those that enjoy it. Unlikely, I think: the opposite is more plausible. My suspicion is that while we have the imitation of low inflation, the government may be tempted to get on the fast track to EMU. This would involve us not merely joining the 2.25 per cent band, but binding ourselves in practice even more closely to the central target exchange rate – along with The Netherlands, Belgium, Luxembourg and perhaps France. Our apron strings to Germany would be measured in millimetres. And we shall be all teed-up for a monetary union. Whatever the Bundesbank does, so shall we do. Their recession or inflation will be ours also. We shall be married to Germany, France and others of the Schengen gang – and divorce will be far too costly for anyone to contemplate.

But unlike the undervalued wife, sterling will be chronically overvalued against the Deutschemark, like the lira and the franc. Britain's remarkably successful export record of the Thatcher years will become, like that of France, mediocre or poor. But the most disturbing result is likely to be the chronic and persistently high level of long-term unemployment. France, Italy, Ireland, The Netherlands, Belgium, Spain – all suffer from chronically high unemployment which has persisted throughout the 1980s. As unemployment rises inexorably, Britain will be emulating its European partners. (I find it remarkable that the countries of the Community have been so tolerant of these high levels of unemployment.)

There is an interesting question whether Britain will join the Italian-Spanish group (not to mention Portugal and Greece) or the French-German group – the fast track or the slow lane. Italy and Spain, besides having high unemployment, also suffer persistent inflation rates above those of France and Germany. I suspect that, even to the Europhile eyes of the *Economist*, the Walters Critique applies at least a little to Italy and Spain. They are caught on the roller coaster with persistently high unemployment and inflation. Will Britain join them? I wish I could say confidently that it will not. But even so, the alternative of emulating the rather miserable experience of the real economy of France in the ERM should not be in the prayers of the people of Britain. I cannot offer the comfort of the *Economist* and the *Financial Times*.

After this experience of ERM, are we nearer to EMU? I believe we are, but only in the sense that Germany's fall from grace has made it much easier for its acolytes to hang on to their pegs. Paradoxically, the idea of one currency and one central bank for Europe has receded, even become a mirage. As I argued a year ago, the Bundesbank will not concede its awesome powers to any new untried central bank of Europe (CBE), and it will only convey those powers if the central bank of Europe has the reputation and authority of the Bundesbank. But without the powers, it has no chance of acquiring the aura of the Bundesbank. The Maastricht constitution of the CBE also has a fatal flaw, which has been highlighted by the Bundesbank. While *domestic* policy is the responsibility of the CBE, whose major objective is to be that of price stability, the Treaty insists that *international* monetary policy, by which it means exchange rate management *inter alia*, will be the responsibility of the *political* authorities. This, of course, allocates more powers than are available. If one controls the exchange rate, then monetary policy follows as a residual. And if, *per contra*, one regulates monetary growth or interest rates, then the exchange rate follows as a residual. It makes sense to vest all powers, both exchange rate and domestic monetary policies, in the CBE. It may well be that the reluctance of the political authorities to cede international monetary policy to the CBE will be the sticking-point for the Bundesbank, and they will, rightly, refuse to be part of such a charade.

On reflection, however, you may fear or hope that the mighty Bundesbank will be overruled by the Chancellor and the German federal government. This has happened before – notably on German reunification. The independence of the Bundesbank was compromised, and there is no guarantee that if the political stakes are high enough, it will not be ignored yet again. The Bundesbank may be forced by the government of the Federal Republic into a union with a brand new untried and untested Central Bank of Europe, perhaps even a CBE that has no control over international monetary policy.

I do fear that this politically dominated outcome is much more likely than I used to believe until recently. The lesson of the Community is the primacy of politics. The thrust to one money is, as I argue earlier in this volume, the spearhead of the Delors plan for the political unification of Europe. It is easier to obtain a consensus on monetary convergence and union than it is to rustle up a convincing commitment to a centralised system of Euro-government and politics. So I believe that the political pressure on Germany and on the Bundesbank will be considerable. As for Britain and the other less reluctant monetary unionists, once we have been encased in the ERM for some five or six years and are pegged within an inch of the mark, it will seem chauvinist – even childish – not to go the whole hog to a full union with one currency.

Finally, with tongue firmly in cheek, I can offer a *theoretical* solution to the dilemmas of monetary union – namely that the Bundesbank becomes the central bank of Europe and we all adopt the Deutschemark as the currency. Then, indeed, the whole of Europe would acquire what was so earnestly sought, namely the credibility of the Bundesbank for their own medium of exchange. Over the last five years, I have regularly put forward this suggestion; it has been received, Germany excepted, with mixtures of incredulity and outrage. Of course it is a political non-starter. The French want to control German monetary policy and, unable to control it through the Bundesbank or via the political process, they see their main hope in creating, and controlling, a central bank of Europe. And if it does come to pass that the CBE comes into being, then I believe that we shall see it much influenced, if not dominated, by the French. In Europe and elsewhere the French bureaucrat has shown his paces and, in my view, is the most able of all Europe's civil servants. (Compare, for example, Roy Jenkins and Jacques Delors.) One may take a view – whether good or bad – about the likely dominance of France in the CBE; here I am concerned with trying to forecast the form of monetary union rather than attempt an evaluation of that form.

What will European policy look like with certainly France and now perhaps Italy and Britain having more control over European monetary policy than they now have in the Deutschemark hegemony? I am afraid it is anyone's guess, and that makes me, at least, rather apprehensive.

9 *Patrick Minford*

The price of monetary unification

Many of us, and businessmen in particular, are enthusiastic that the European Project goes ahead successfully. Business benefits from a Single Market, and the sooner that it can safely enjoy the benefits of a Single Currency, the better. The more government co-operation there is in removing the innumerable - often hidden - barriers to business in Europe, whether they be different standards, complicated tax adjustments across borders, or public preferences for home producers, the better.

But we must be careful that what is built in Europe is truly an improvement on what we have. There are many forms that closer links and co-operation may take, just as an architect has access to a variety of possible plans for a building. In other chapters we have discussed some of the difficulties surrounding the present Delors blueprint for European integration, such as the interventionist Social Charter, the flawed and costly Common Agricultural Policy, and the protectionist use of anti-dumping. These are examples of foolish and dangerous interference, which could well backfire and lead to less co-operation in practice.

In this chapter I focus on monetary co-operation in Europe. We would all like the following good things from the monetary regimes we follow in Europe:

stable exchange rates;

stable prices;

stable employment and output; and

stable interest rates.

The question is, what is the best way to get them, or a reasonable combination of them?

Basically there are two main possibilities:

i. to fix exchange rates, starting with the Exchange Rate Mechanism (ERM) and moving on to Monetary Union: a Single Currency with some central EEC authority printing money and fixing interest rates for all;

ii. to let each country fix its own interest rates and print its own money: to co-operate with the others, taking account of the effects their monetary policies have on each other, but letting exchange rates be flexible.

Faced with two stark alternatives the British reaction is typically to say: there must be a compromise - a third way! Not so. Either you fix or you flex your exchange rate: if you have a fixed-but-adjustable exchange rate you get into a mess, with great instability (unless you suppress it with tough exchange controls, which are worse). The first reason is that the foreign exchange markets speculate against your currency when fixed, betting on a devaluation (a safe one-way option bet, because if there is no devaluation they do not lose). There are other problems too: there is an inconsistency between allowing a country no freedom to adjust its interest rates in the short term because it must protect its exchange rate, and yet allowing it full freedom in the long term when its exchange rate can freely move.

These problems were only too apparent in the early European experiments with fixing exchange rates. First there was the 'Snake' set up after the Werner Report in the early 1970s. It allowed frequent parity adjustments and it soon collapsed under the weight of speculation. The ERM of the 1980s was also of this compromise sort, but parity changes had to be agreed; nevertheless, there were severe policy conflicts between the ERM's principles of fixity and the monetary desires of members. The most vivid example was France under Mitterrand's 'dash for growth' in the early 1980s; it devalued a total of 45 per cent against the Dm. Italy too devalued sharply, by nearly 60 per cent. The ERM nearly broke down.

Our research group in Liverpool examined the potential instability for this type of ERM, using the technique of 'stochastic simulation' where you pepper an economic model of the EEC with repeated typical shocks and compare the variability of the economy under different monetary regimes. We found indeed that this sort of ERM was likely to exhibit considerably higher instability than floating, especially if there were no attempts to coordinate monetary policies of the EEC members. In the light of such instability the EEC was forced to move in one or other direction - back to floating or on to fixed. It moved towards more and more fixity; since 1987 there have been effectively no devaluations within the ERM. Finally the logic of this movement has driven it to monetary union (EMU) itself.

Let us consider this process in two stages: the transitional period of the 'tight ERM' and the final stage of EMU, irrevocably fixed exchange rates and the single money. The problem with tight ERM is that there is very little flexibility in interest rates as in the exchange rate. Interest rates must be set to defend the exchange rate, which can barely move. The result is that interest rates may well be inappropriate for domestic needs, while the currency may get out of line with domestic costs and create international uncompetitiveness. These problems are clearly illustrated by Britain's recent experience. In early 1988, when we were only 'shadow' ERM members, we kept the pound down against the Dm and pulled interest rates right down to that end - they reached 7.5 per cent in the spring - with the result that we had an uncontrolled boom that year. Then from mid 1990, as we talked the pound up into joining by October, interest rates were held high to keep it up at our chosen rate of Dm 2.95. Yet by then the economy was in free fall. By holding interest rates at 15 per cent, and then 14 per cent until mid-February, with only grudging falls afterwards, the recession has been prolonged and has truly become a slump.

The pound is also overvalued, as is clear from the continued current account deficit even in the present depths of the recession. Yet an even more cautionary tale is available from Italy, whose failure to devalue since 1987, combined with steady inflation well above Germany's, has led to an overvaluation we estimate at around 30 per cent. Italy copes with this by subsidies, both overt and hidden, to its trading industries. But subsidies create inefficiency and a poor allocation of resources.

Some economists have argued that these problems would be largely resolved if exchange rates were irrevocably fixed. Then wages and prices would be under maximum pressure to come into line as devaluation could never bail out domestic industries. Interest rates too would be equal at some average European level: neither too high nor too low, provided there was a sound European central bank.

This view has carried much weight with the Commission, which has accordingly pushed for rapid moves to EMU. I now therefore turn to a consideration of the problems of EMU itself, which I believe this view greatly underestimates.

The shackles of monetary union

Every schoolboy knows the advantages in principle of a common currency, even if he has never travelled abroad. In November 1990 the EEC Commission (1990) made a heroic attempt to measure them. Their efforts ran to 351 pages, and they suggested that the efficiency gain from removing currency uncertainty and exchange costs might be worth as much as 10 per cent of EEC GNP! Virtually all of this, however, comes from the effect of a supposed reduction in the risk premium on the cost of capital, on which more anon. The various other gains adduced from the common currency included those of increased price stability (especially through enhanced credibility), more disciplined public finance, and greater macroeconomic stability.

However, price stability is attainable with or without EMU, as is credibility. Whether EMU makes them more easily attainable is a matter of political economy, which is not tackled by the EEC's report: what will be the Euro-Fed's powers and incentives to preserve a stable currency, as opposed to those of existing monetary authorities? These questions raise wide considerations and are not easily settled. We will not pursue them in this chapter, but merely note that there are strong arguments to suggest that agreement between twelve democratic governments on a Euro-Bank devoted solely to tight money and unaccountable to the participating democracies is unattainable. The assumption that such a Euro-Bank will be as reliable as the Bundesbank is precisely that: an assumption - one, moreover, of extreme doubtfulness. The arguments that arise on this issue are not addressed in the EEC report.

By discipline on public finance seems to be meant the inability of a regional government to raise taxation through *seigniorage* - that is, through printing money and causing inflation, which can be classified as a form of taxation (sometimes also called the 'inflation tax'). A virtue is made of what is generally regarded as a problem. On certain occasions (such as wars, when the costs of raising orthodox tax are high), it is fiscally optimal to print money and use the inflation tax. Yet the EEC report makes a virtue out of denying regional governments access to this tax. Again, we will not pursue this matter here, other than briefly to illustrate it from the parlous financial state of the Italian government. Since it joined the Exchange Rate Mechanism on a tight basis (no devaluation, etc.) it has effectively lost its powers to levy a sizeable inflation tax on the otherwise tax-free zone of the shadow economy, especially in the South. Whatever else the new tight ERM has done for Italy, it has made the prospect of reaching budget balance much more distant, if indeed it has not disappeared altogether: the Italian government goes on borrowing at an overvalued exchange rate, where foreign exchange intervention within the ERM keeps down the prospect of devaluation and so holds down interest rates. So its borrowing is subsidised and yet shows no sign of slowing: already public debt exceeds 100 per cent of national income. The EEC report offers no mechanisms, only pious hopes, for achieving movement to fiscal balance under EMU. No *seigniorage* and no alternative fiscal mechanism: it hardly seems to constitute a fiscal improvement.

The last claim by the EEC report, of greater macro stability, will be looked at below under 'Stabilisation gains and losses'; it constitutes our main agenda in this chapter.

Analytically, the efficiency gain claimed by the EEC report comes from removing the transaction costs of currency exchange and the costs of guarding against currency uncertainty. There are three qualitative arguments which suggest that its 'guesstimate' of 10 per cent is absurdly high:

(1) Currency risk can essentially be 'diversified away', in a world of many currencies and investment vehicles whose risks are correlated with currency risk. Hence the cost of insuring against it ('hedging') should be driven down to zero.

(2) A transaction involving currency exchange should not, on the face of it (given the negligible cost of keying in electronic orders), cost any more in credit transactions than an ordinary transaction in home currency, other than the cost of hedging net balances in any one currency between clearings.

Both these considerations suggest that the only saving comes in the exchange of notes and coin. But this is extremely limited: notes and coin are generally (with one or two exceptions such as Italy) a small percentage of Gross Domestic Product (GDP), and that part of it which is exchanged for foreign notes and coin is a small percentage of that again.

The EEC Commission's estimate of the transactions cost saving on its own - not to be confused with the currency uncertainty saving just discussed - is a mere 0.4 per cent of GDP. Indeed, the report suggests that it is heavily concentrated among the smaller countries with less sophisticated banking systems; in countries like the UK it would be about 0.1 per cent of GDP. These estimates of transactions cost are based on a survey of financial firms' commission charges, and these are applied to estimates of the volume of business attracting these charges. They seem entirely reasonable, but their minimal size must be carefully borne in mind.

(3) If the gain were as large as the full EEC guesstimate, then other pairs of nations enjoying a similar degree of inter-trade would have surely actively considered a common currency. Yet the countries of EFTA, of North America, of Eastern Europe, to name but a few candidates, have never seemed to put this idea seriously on the treaty agenda.

This last point suggests that, whatever the truth in the EEC Commission's estimate, the key point in inducing nations to have a common currency must lie elsewhere, in the balance of other gains and losses. Indeed, it is that assumption that lies behind the extensive literature on the 'optimal common currency area'; that literature invokes a variety of criteria - for example, the degree of labour and capital mobility, and the extent of fiscal transfers - but the extent of foreign exchange transactions does not figure importantly among them, though there must be a presumption that there will be some gain from reduced currency transaction costs.

Our purpose here is to examine this balance of other gains and losses, and specifically those coming from the loss of a flexible exchange rate and so of national monetary policy in reacting to repeated economic shocks – what we shall loosely call the 'stabilisation' aspect.

Stabilisation gains and losses

In evaluating the stabilisation aspect for any given single currency proposal, we must make assumptions about the institutional framework. It makes a lot of difference whether there is a high degree of labour mobility, and what arrangements there are for regional transfers from the central budget.

In the case of the EEC, it has been noted by Eichengreen (1990) that less than 1 per cent of any national or regional decline in GDP is compensated by transfers from the central Community budget (as against 30 per cent from the US federal budget); nor are there any plans to raise this 'offset coefficient' to any number remotely comparable with the US one. The Delors Committee (Delors, 1989) called merely for a doubling, but even that may not be agreed by the nations that would have to double their fiscal contribution to Brussels.

Labour mobility is also limited, for the vast bulk of nationals in the richer countries of the EEC. The key reason appears to be language and cultural differences, which make a French citizen, for instance, pause before resettling in Frankfurt. Significant migration is mostly from the poorer countries to the richer, as immigration controls that normally stop this have been invalidated. But even this mobility is not large because capital mobility within the free EEC market enables workers in poor countries such as Spain, parts of the UK and Southern Italy, on the 'periphery' of the EEC, to attract investment and enjoy improved wages without the cost of moving. Capital mobility and free trade thus work as alternatives for labour mobility, an idea central to the trade theories of Eli Heckscher and Bertil Ohlin. We assume here that trade is free even if '1992' has not yet fully come through and may not do so until the next century. We also assume that capital is perfectly mobile within the Community and that there are no exchange controls.

As the optimum currency area argument emphasises, it is obvious that whatever stabilisation task is performed by flexible exchange rates and divergent monetary policy, it can be partially performed by either labour mobility or fiscal transfers. To that extent, the EEC is handicapped in its bid to be an optimum currency area. Our calculations below reflect this handicap. (If EMU goes ahead regardless, that might well lead to demands for further progress on fiscal policy and labour mobility, but that is another matter.)

Our methodology: 'stochastic simulation' of Liverpool models

The technique of 'stochastic simulation' involves applying numerous shocks of a nature found in the past to a model that simulates the world economy, and seeing how stable in various respects the simulated world economy turns out to be. The idea is like that of a flight simulator where a model (a set of equations describing the behaviour of an aircraft) is used to compute reactions to the aviator and the environment because it is impractical or dangerous to check these reactions experimentally.

Before proceeding to apply this technique to EMU and floating exchange rates, we should note an argument frequently made by those in favour of EMU: that monetary arrangements as such should alter not the equilibrium state of the real economy, merely national price levels. Our approach here is straightforward. We agree, and the Liverpool models explicitly assume, that real equilibria are immune to monetary arrangements. But our model features a variety of ways in which short-run behaviour differs under different monetary arrangements. This is because prices, wages and interest rates are fixed by people with out-of-date or imperfect information about monetary forces or subject to a variety of long-term contracts. So when monetary and other shocks hit the economy, it takes time for all these prices to reflect accurately the true pressures on the economy.

The Liverpool models have been estimated over both fixed and floating periods, and appear to have reasonable stability across this particular regime change (for example, Minford, Ioannidis and Marwaha, 1983). To this extent they should be serviceable for our study here, which can be thought of as comparing floating rates with stages 2 and 3 of the Delors proposals (Delors, 1989), where currencies are 'irrevocably' pegged with a trivial margin (1 per cent - stage 2) or none at all (stage 3). They cannot be used with as much confidence to evaluate a Europe in which there is the single currency itself - but they may be the nearest we can get with our present econometric technology. One should remember nevertheless that even after a common currency is established, it is in principle possible for any sovereign country to withdraw from it later. It would require the cessation of national sovereignty and, therefore, complete political union to guarantee totally against secession; so perhaps EMU and stages 2 and 3 are not so distinct as might at first appear.

Evaluating the cost of fixing exchange rates

When exchange rates are completely fixed, then in the conditions of perfect capital mobility assumed in our models, national monetary policy is entirely impotent and some rule must be invoked for the single monetary authority in charge within the currency area. Formally, therefore, we can treat this as equivalent *de facto* to a single currency area (with the caveat mentioned above that if the latter were to be 'more irrevocable' than merely pegged rates, behaviour and therefore the coefficients in the model could change).

How either floating or EMU behaves in the face of shocks depends on how monetary policy behaves. We distinguish two main possibilities: money supply targets pursued without response to shocks ('fixed money'), and continuous money supply optimisation in response to events, including those produced by other countries' responses ('strategic money'). Under EMU, clearly the latter monetary response is the result of some sort of co-operation between EEC countries; to model this we assume that the preferences of the four leading countries (France, Germany, Italy and the UK) are given an equal weight in this co-operative decision-making.

The tables that follow show 'welfare costs' produced by a large number of shocks typical over the sample period (from the mid-sixties to the mid-eighties). These welfare costs are weighted averages of the variances (squared effects of the shocks) of output, prices, real interest rates, the real exchange rate (i.e. competitiveness), and the growth rate of the money supply. The weights are designed to give an equal penalty to a 1 per cent effect on each (1 per cent per annum in the case of the real interest rate) and 3 per cent per annum for the money supply. Each simulation works by a set of shocks being applied to a 'base forecast'. The effects, in terms of the deviation of output, etc. from the base forecast, are then computed and squared. These are then weighted and added up to create the welfare cost for that particular set of shocks. The procedure is repeated for many different sets of shocks (each shock is a random drawing for a specific type of shock, such as higher real wage demands or larger investment spending). The total result - the (total) welfare cost, or 'cost' for short -is shown in the tables.

Table 9.1 shows the costs of these two regimes under the assumption that countries not within the ERM or EMU choose independent money supply growth rates to minimise their welfare costs subject to the choices of others: the 'strategic money' assumption described above. Under floating, the EEC countries each also behave in this way. Under EMU, Germany is assumed to set its money supply, minimising EEC joint welfare costs - a coalition differing from ERM through the absence of any margins of intra-EEC currency fluctuation at all. (We assume that ERM is not under discussion here: it is regarded as a poor substitute for EMU, as indeed we found it to be in a previous paper, see

Table 9.1 Welfare Costs of EMU *vs.* Floating*

	EMU	*Floating*	*Preferred Regime*
EC			
Germany	0.2	1.8	EMU
France	0.4	0.9	EMU
Italy	0.5	41.6	EMU
United Kingdom	0.6	0.2	Floating
Rest of World			
United States	1.6	1.0	Floating
Canada	20.3	47.4	EMU
Japan	3.6	6.8	EMU

*Each number is the welfare cost (a 'bad') as defined in the text. The larger it is the larger the instability produced by the many different shocks interacting with the regime examined.

Table 9.2 Joint EEC Welfare costs of feasible EEC regimes*

	Fixed money	*Indep. money*	*Various coalitions in EEC* ALL	Ex-UK	Ex-FR	Ex-IT	*World Co-op.*
Floating	3.0	44.5	1.1	13.2	209.2	5.6	2.2
EMU	4.8	-	1.8	2.2	4.4	3.2	5.0

*See note to Table 9.1.

Hughes Hallett *et al.*, 1990). It can be seen from Table 9.1 that if this is the relevant choice set, then the EEC countries will not agree on which regime is best. Germany, France and Italy prefer EMU, the UK prefers floating. In case other countries' preferences have any influence, they too can be seen to differ, with the US urging floating on the EEC and Japan and Canada urging EMU.

Beside this money supply regime, it would be possible to imagine completely fixed money supplies (the 'fixed money' assumption discussed above), or money supplies co-ordinated worldwide to minimise joint world welfare costs. Of course, the first is not generally practised, while the second would require international agreement which is currently absent. However unlikely, all these regimes are shown in Table 9.2 with the joint welfare costs of EEC countries that result from them. A rational way for the EEC to choose a regime would be to settle on that exchange rate and monetary regime combination which minimised their joint welfare costs; then side-payments (or equivalent compensation) could be made to those who lose out. Table 9.2 reveals that the optimum is a coalition of all EC countries for the management of their money supplies but under floating rates. The next best is EMU: but it is substantially (64%) more unstable than this cooperative float. This result comes out as plainly if one examines the variability of output and prices alone, as is often done. Figure 9.1 shows how much greater the variability of both is under EMU than under floating, especially if monetary policy can be used cooperatively in the floating case.

Figure 9.1 Liverpool model estimates of price and output variability under EMU and floating (variability measured by standard deviation).

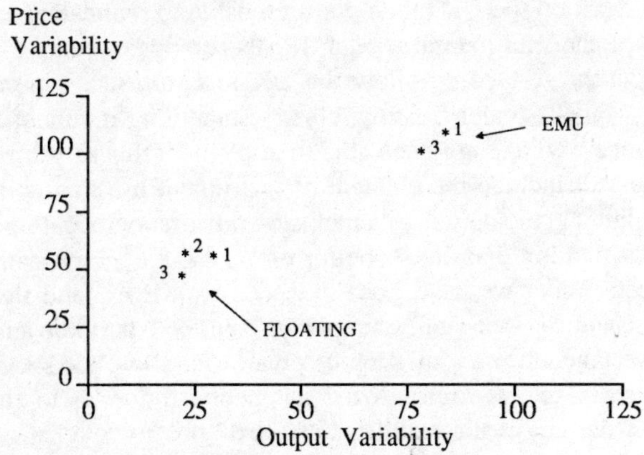

Key: 1 – Money supply fixed,
2 – Non-cooperative monetary policy response
3 – Cooperative monetary policy response

Source: Minford, Rastogi and Hughes Hallett, 1992.

It would seem, therefore, that the global optimum for the EEC is to float but to co-ordinate monetary policies.

A careful look at the UK alone

The above calculations are done in a multilateral context, using our multilateral Liverpool world model (Minford, Agenor and Nowell, 1986). This allows us to study both the fixed money and the strategic money cases. Inevitably a model such as our world model built with annual data is not, as we have found from our work on the UK, as empirically reliable as one estimated on quarterly data, because there are fewer degrees of freedom in annual data. Accordingly, we set out to test the annual results on our Liverpool quarterly model of the UK (Minford, Matthews and Rastogi, 1990). We can do this only for fixed money at present, but this at least gives us a limited comparison of results with the more elaborate exercise on the multilateral world model.

In the work on the UK model we are unable to replicate the strategic analysis of the multilateral model, for the obvious reason that it is a single country. We could allow the UK to optimise its monetary response to shocks under floating, clearly something it cannot do under EMU. Since we have not been able to implement this as yet, our calculations do not include the element of instrument use that is present in the multilateral calculations; its inclusion must favour floating, because it is under floating that the scope for use of the monetary instrument is the widest. What we have done is to compare EMU and floating for the UK, assuming that money supply is fixed, both at home and abroad. Hence we take German inflation as given (but allow for shocks to the German real exchange rate). What this exercise does is to check how important the automatic stabiliser effect of floating exchange rates is for the UK. Details of our methods are given in Minford *et al.* (1992).

We can divide our analysis into two parts: the effects of shocks on UK behavioural equations (consumption, wages, etc.) and the effects on variables given externally to the model, both domestic and foreign. The former part can be thought of as the uncertainty arising if government policy and the world environment is totally stable. With the latter part, one might expect floating to be superior, because under EMU there is a greater propensity to import foreign shocks. With regard to the former, it could go either way. For example, with prices it would depend on how behavioural shocks affected the real exchange rate and so prices under EMU, or on the demand for money and so prices under floating. In fact, it turns out that price uncertainty is important in determining overall instability in this model, so that this also will determine stability for other variables.

It can be seen from the first two columns of Table 9.3 that there is not a great deal of difference in the response of floating and EMU to UK behavioural shocks. The capacity to stabilise is roughly the same. EMU actually stabilises the price level somewhat better, while floating has a slight superiority in stabilising each of inflation, output and unemployment. But as these things go there is really nothing in it. Once we include policy and world shocks, the picture changes markedly. The volatility of the price level under EMU depends on the volatility of the real exchange rate of Germany as well as of the UK. We have assumed that German monetary policy succeeds in totally stabilising the German price level through its monetary policy rule. But of course EMU cannot stabilise Germany's real exchange rate against the world as a whole; we have assumed its volatility to be about the same as during the past two decades. UK domestic policy shocks that affect the real exchange rate, and especially supply-side shocks, can also be a considerable source of economic variability.

Table 9.3 Standard deviation of key variables, over eight years (shocks applied in first four): floating and EMU in the UK, under fixed money worldwide–Liverpool model of UK

	Behavioural Shocks		*Policy Shocks*		*World Shocks*		*All Shocks*	
	Float	*EMU*	*Float*	*EMU*	*Float*	*EMU*	*Float*	*EMU*
GDP (% of 1990)	18.3	20.1	5.1	7.6	0.4	15.1	18.4	24.6
GDP growth (%)	27.3	26.9	4.4	5.3	0.5	4.0	27.1	26.6
Price level (% of 1990)	17.1	6.6	12.8	19.9	1.5	36.0	20.3	49.1
Inflation(%)	5.6	6.6	5.2	13.2	0.6	7.9	7.4	17.7
Interest rate (short-term,%)	5.6	0.8	8.5	1.5	1.1	2.1	9.9	2.4
Real exchange rate (%)	11.5	9.7	30.6	28.6	2.9	50.2	32.1	63.2
Unemployment (%)	16.7	18.0	1.6	1.3	0.2	1.0	10.3	11.0
Misery index (Inflation + Unemployment)	22.3	24.6	6.8	14.5	0.8	8.9	17.7	28.7

Table 9.4 Ratio of standard deviation in second four years to that in first four years

	Floating	*EMU*
GDP	0.31	0.97
Growth	0.12	0.25
Price level	1.36	2.14
Inflation	0.47	0.54
Interest rate	0.13	0.73
Real exchange rate	0.65	2.11
Unemployment	0.04	0.08

Both these sorts of shocks are stabilised by a floating rate in their effects on prices, because monetary conditions determine prices. There is therefore some reason to suppose that floating will give more stability in the face of policy and external shocks than EMU. This indeed turns out to be the case. Though growth under EMU is of similar stability, and nominal interest rates are much more stable under EMU, the output level and all other nominal variables are destabilised by EMU. The results indicate that shocks produce larger and more persistent deviations of both price level and output under EMU than under floating. (The greater persistence is confirmed by the ratio of the standard error in the second four years to that in the first four when the shocks come in: see Table 9.4.) The additional instability under EMU comes largely from its greater vulnerability to world shocks, especially of course the Dm's real volatility, but policy (supply-side) shocks contribute importantly too. To world shocks, floating gives almost complete protection, so that EMU's performance is proportionally very much worse; but the deterioration of the misery index under supply-side shocks is over 100 per cent.

Across all shocks, therefore, this poor performance on policy and world shocks means that floating gives substantially less instability than EMU. There is a 60 per cent deterioration in the overall misery index in EMU relative to floating.

Conclusions

The results I have been discussing are no more than common sense would suggest. One does not have to be a Keynesian to believe that there is enough short-run nominal rigidity in wages and prices to cause adjustment difficulties in the face of differential national shocks, which a floating rate can ease through its total flexibility. Exchange markets react instantly, with forward-looking expectations, to shocks, while wages and prices react slowly, slowed by contract and information lags. This is the essential reason for the superiority of floating over EMU. We have found it to be true for all EEC countries that they benefit from floating rather than EMU; for the UK, the gain is particularly large, presumably because of its particularly large external links outside the EEC – links that in an ideal world most decidedly ought to persist and be built upon.

A previous piece of conventional wisdom (e.g. Macdougall, 1977) was that a common currency in Europe would require large-scale fiscal transfers to compensate regions and nations for these costs. The new EEC Commission wisdom is that there are no significant costs of this sort to set against the massive benefits they claim from higher efficiency in exchange; the small EC regional funds are sufficient to achieve 'solidarity'. But as we have seen, there is every reason to disbelieve the Commission's claims.

Instead, I would argue that the gains from a single currency (essentially those of lower transactions costs) will only outweigh the costs we have been discussing when there is a much higher degree of economic integration, much like that between Wales and England. Then shocks will be sufficiently similar greatly to lower the need for relative price movements, while the disruption from money-changing for cross-border transactions would become obviously substantial. At this point we would say that we are dealing with an 'optimum currency area'. But for many countries of the EEC this degree of integration is a long way off. For now, most countries should be looking for flexible arrangements and co-operation in monetary relations within Europe.

As for the Dutch proposals for monetary union adopted at the Maastricht Summit in December 1991, they are on this view infinitely preferable to those of M. Delors and his committee which called for a rigid timetable for moves to monetary union, with irrevocably fixed exchange rates by the mid 1990s. The Dutch proposals, if used incautiously, could permit premature movement to monetary union. But they can also be used to slow it down, if the UK and others insist on the criteria for convergence being rigorously applied. The UK itself and others can stay out of any single currency; others can be prevented from joining by lack of convergence. In this way, only those countries that are highly integrated might go ahead, either within the Treaty or outside it. That would be the right way to proceed.

As I argued at the start, the convenience to business of a single currency is something to obtain as early as it can safely be done. But safety requires caution and evolution. Most countries of the EEC, including the UK, are not ready for it yet.

Note

1. I am grateful to Patrick Robertson for useful discussions and to Ralph Harris for most helpful and detailed comments on an earlier draft.

References

Delors, J. (1989) *Report on Economic and Monetary Union in the European Community*, European Commission, *The Delors Report*, Office for Official Publications of the EC, Luxembourg.

Eichengreen, B. (1990) 'One money for Europe? Lessons from the US currency union', *Economic Policy*, April 1990, pp. 117-89.

European Commission (1990) 'One market, one money - an evaluation of the potential benefits and costs of forming an economic and monetary union', *European Economy*, no. 44, October.

Hughes Hallett, A., P. Minford and A. Rastogi (1990) *The European Monetary System: Achievements and Survival*, Working paper no. 90/04, Liverpool Research Group in Macroeconomics.

MacDougall, Sir Donald (1977) *Public Finance in European Integration: The MacDougall Report*, EC Commission, , Office for Official Publications of the EC, Luxembourg.

Minford, P., C. Ioannidis and S. Marwaha (1983) 'Dynamic predictive tests of a model under adaptive and rational expectations', *Economic Letters*, II, pp. 115-21.

Minford, P., K. Matthews, and A. Rastogi (1990) *A quarterly version of the Liverpool model of the UK*, working paper no. 90/06, Liverpool Research Group in Macroeconomics.

Minford, P., P. Agenor and E. Nowell (1986) 'A New Classical econometric model of the world economy', *Economic Modelling*, 3, pp. 154-74.

Minford, P., A. Rastogi and A. Hughes Hallett (1992) 'The price of EMU Revisited', working paper No. 656, Centre for Economic Policy Research, London; revised version of Minford and Rastogi 'The Price of Emu', in *Britain and EMU* (ed. R. Dornbusch and R. Layard), Centre for Economic Performance in assoc. with Financial Markets Group, LSE, December 1990.

10 *B. C. Roberts*

The Social Charter

The promotion of a Charter of Fundamental Social Rights was an astute political move by Jacques Delors, President of the European Commission, which aimed at extending the limited mention of social issues in the Treaty of Rome without a revision of the Treaty. Delors' principal purpose was to win popular support for a major increase in the role of the Community in the social field, and to present a challenge to dominant free-market principles. As a socialist he believed that, after the boost these principles had been given by the Single European Act, the social effects on workers would require increased protective regulation, and that it was the duty of the Community to provide this.

The Treaty of Rome makes provision for the setting of standards within the Community of health and safety at work. It also calls for the observation of the 'principle of equal pay for equal work'. Apart from these two issues, and the ensuring of the rights of free movement of workers, the Treaty does not call specifically for legislation in the social field.

The Treaty, in Article 118, does, however, list the following areas where 'the Commission shall have the task of promoting close cooperation between Member States in the social field': employment; labour law and working conditions; basic and advanced vocational training; social security; prevention of occupational accidents and diseases; occupational hygiene; the right of association and collective bargaining between employers and workers. 'To this end the Commission shall act in close contact with Member States by making studies, delivering opinions and arranging consultations both on problems arising at the national level and on those of concern to international organisations.'

Delors' objective was to go beyond Article 118 as it had been amended by Article 119a, which had been adopted as part of the Single

European Act. This confined the imposing of directives to the health and safety of workers. By using the Charter as a device, not provided for in the Treaty, he aimed to secure the commitment of member states to a social action programme that could be given effect by scores of directives, going well beyond what was possible under the amended Treaty. He hoped to secure unanimous approval for the Charter which, as a solemn declaration, member states would accept as having binding effect when they were called upon to vote for the necessary directives.

Delors did not secure the unanimous vote he asked for, but only Britain voted against. Under this dubious cloak of legitimacy the Commission announced a social action programme consisting of forty-seven measures to give effect to the first stage of the Social Charter. Since many of these proposals were subject to the unanimity rule which would give Britain, which is not bound by the Charter, an opportunity to exercise its veto, Mrs Vasso Papandreou (the Commissioner heading the Directorate for Employment, Industrial Relations and Social Affairs, DG5) stated that whenever possible the limitation of the Treaty would be evaded by bringing directives forward under the Health and Safety clause.

It was subsequently decided by the Commission to try to secure in the Maastricht Treaty a chapter embodying the objectives of the Social Charter which would include a considerable extension of qualified majority voting. Following powerful resistance by Britain to this proposal, it was eventually agreed that the social chapter should not be a clause of the revised treaty, but a protocol which authorised the eleven other member states to make agreements implementing the chapter, but without British participation.

Delors' reasons why the Community should adopt common standards of social rights.

M. Delors and Mrs Papandreou have argued that the Community must be more than just a free trade area: it must be a 'people's Community'. On this view the Social Charter is essential to secure and maintain the support of the people for the activities of the Community. 'Europe cannot be built against the opinions of the employers or workers or of the general public; it needs the full participation of all social groups. In this context, we must not ignore the fact that there is growing discontent on the part of the general public with the single market.'

The Commission has sought to justify this opinion by reference to the results of its Eurobarometer surveys which have shown that more than two-thirds of the sample have been in favour of a common set of rules concerning the rights and responsibilities of workers and employers. This is not surprising, since high scores for general propositions which appear to provide costless benefits to those answering questionnaires are not unusual. When it comes, however, to specific propositions which include the costs, the response is often quite different, especially in different member states.

If we turn to more substantive reasons given by Delors for the Community to adopt the Social Charter, the first was that it is necessary in order to prevent the benefits of the Single Market going primarily to employers and other wealthy capitalists. A second reason was that a common pattern of social protection, initiated and monitored by the Commission, would contribute to the achievement of a 'level playing field' in terms of social costs and benefits, which differ considerably between member states. A third reason was that harmonisation of social standards would deepen the role of the central organs of the Community, thus contributing to the achievement of a federal union of member states. A fourth reason for the social action programme was that it would lead to an improvement in efficiency, as well as fairness, within the Community since harmonisation would be based on the principle of best practice. A fifth reason advanced was the need to strengthen the trade unions as principal partners with employers in the social dialogue and in collective bargaining, which the Commission believed should be a central feature of decision-making in the sphere of employment.

In judging the validity of the case for the adoption of the Social Charter it is necessary to examine these arguments put forward by Delors and DG5.

Will the Single Market primarily benefit the wealthy?

Fear that the establishment of the Single Market will primarily benefit wealthy capitalists is rooted in the classic beliefs of socialists that this is the way a liberal market economy works. It was a fundamental theory of Marx that a free labour market would inevitably result in the exploitation of labour and the degeneration of living standards. It followed that this could only be prevented by the expropriation of the capitalist class, with the means of production, distribution and exchange placed in the hands of the state. This theory, though demonstrably wrong, has had a tremendous influence on European socialist parties and their trade union offsprings, though they have ceased to believe in the necessity of revolution, accepting instead the need for a substantial degree of state ownership and state regulation of the economy. Christian socialist doctrines, of which M. Delors, a former French trade union leader, is a leading exponent, have their roots in Christian teaching which is also hostile to the operation of a free market, but shuns any violent solution (except in Latin America), seeking instead social dialogue and social regulation.

The authors of the Treaty of Rome were clearly influenced more by Adam Smith and the classical economists than by any strand of socialist thought. However, while the Treaty mentions social policy only briefly, in terms of improving employment opportunities, working conditions and other aspects of workers' standards of life, it does so in the context of a statement that: 'They believe that such development will ensue not only from the functioning of the common market which will favour the harmonisation of social systems, but also from the procedures provided for in this Treaty and from the approximation of provisions laid down by law, regulation or administrative action.' This opened up the possibility for socialists, such as M. Delors and Mrs Papandreou, to claim that the Community needed a Social Charter that would strengthen workers' rights in order to ensure that the social aims implicit in this statement were realised.

There is clear evidence from modern political and economic history that the factors which are crucial to raising the living standards of workers are a pluralistic political system and a liberal market economy of the kind envisaged by the authors of the Treaty of Rome and consolidated in the Single European Act. Over the past century the success stories in the improvement of working and living standards have been achieved in countries where these principles predominated. The disasters in terms of poverty and deprivation of liberty, as recent events in Eastern Europe have demonstrated beyond question, have occurred in those countries which have adopted the totalitarian, centralised, bureaucratic systems of socialism. Whilst the European Community is far from being authoritarian, the development of the Community as it is perceived by M. Delors and most socialists would be highly centralised and bureaucratic, and would have a destructive effect on the separate cultural traditions and social, political and economic structures which the member states have severally created over the course of centuries, and which have made a fundamental contribution to the special quality and greatness of European civilisation.

The demonstration across the world that socialism does not provide what its utopian supporters have fervently hoped for does not mean that a modern market economy can be effectively operated without a certain degree of regulation. A democratic capitalist market economy is not synonymous with the creation of a state of anarchy. It is accepted by the most liberal enthusiasts of a market system that an element of regulation is necessary to ensure that trading and social relations are protected from monopolistic cartels and from other means of rigging the market for the benefit of special interest groups, powerful individuals or corporate institutions, public or private . It is also accepted that some regulation of employment conditions is necessary, as well as many other areas of social concern such as health, education, poverty and incapacity to work – to mention some of the most important.

Those who question the need for the Social Charter would not quarrel with the need for action by member states to protect by regulation the social rights of their citizens under all the headings of the Charter listed below, with the need for the Community to be concerned with some of them, such as freedom of movement and health matters.

These headings are: (1) the improvement of living and working conditions; (2) the right to freedom of movement; (3) the right to employment and remuneration; (4) the right to health protection; (5) the protection of children and adolescents; (6) the protection of elderly persons; (7) the protection of disabled persons; (8) social protection; (9) the right to freedom of association and collective bargaining; (10) the right to vocational training; (11) the right of men and women to equal treatment; (12) the right to information, consultation and worker participation.

This list of headings which the Commission wishes to be the subject of regulations to be imposed by the Community are mostly already covered by legislation in all the member states and some by already-enacted Community directives, which the Commission now wishes to extend. They are also covered to a very large extent, if not entirely, by the international conventions of the International Labour Organisation, to which all member states belong, and by the Council of Europe's Social Charter which took effect in 1965 and which, like the International Labour Code, is continuously brought up to date.

It is quite clear the Commission is not interested simply in filling gaps in the extensive range of national laws and international conventions that already exist, but in superseding successful systems by a vast network of new regulations that through their administrative, legal and financial consequences will create a host of difficulties. Since the laws and labour market processes that already exist ensure that the effects of the Single Market will not solely, or even mainly, benefit the wealthy, there is little substance in this argument for the Commission's Social Charter.

The 'level playing field' argument

Another argument which has been advanced in favour of the Social Charter seems at first sight to be based on less ideological grounds. It is that unrestricted competition will lead to what has been termed 'social dumping'. Therefore it is necessary to protect workers and their employers from this effect, which is claimed to be socially harmful.

However, this argument is no more plausible than the previous argument that labour will inevitably be exploited under a Single Market. Market theory suggests that capital will flow to the countries where labour costs (including social benefits) are lowest, and that labour will flow to areas where real wages (including social benefits) are highest and jobs are available. This will mean that workers in the high-wage countries will face competition from an inflow of labour, probably prepared to accept marginally lower wages. Demand for labour in the high-wage areas will also be affected by an increase in competition from goods imported from the lower-cost countries in the Community. The immediate effect of these shifts will be to benefit consumers through lower prices and to increase unemployment in the high-cost countries. As a result of this competition, firms in the higher-labour-cost countries will have lower profits which will encourage them to introduce labour-saving equipment and more efficient methods of production. As profits are restored, investment will be increased, new developments will be undertaken and new fields of employment opportunity created.

This is the classic process of the market and what in fact is taking place all the time where market economies exist. The net effect of these shifts is that, while there is some temporary dislocation as the market adjusts to changes in supply and demand and the introduction of new technology, in the long run the pressure of competition and the adjustment of costs ensures that both less advanced and more advanced countries will grow, and the gap between them will narrow. Employment will recover and most people will be better off.

The most vivid example of this process of market adjustment to the free flows of capital and the free movement of labour is to be seen during the past forty years in the remarkable growth of the economies and living standards of countries such as Japan, Hong Kong, Taiwan, South Korea, Singapore and many others once miserably poor. With access to markets in the more advanced countries, they are now able to match their standards and in some cases surpass them. Some employers and some workers in the advanced countries were adversely affected, but in general the growth of previously backward countries has not been at the expense of the more advanced countries, which have been stimulated by competition into greater economic growth, while enjoying the benefits of high-quality, lower-cost imports. The Third World, too, has benefited enormously from competitive low-cost imports.

The objective behind the advocates of the Social Charter as a means of blocking 'social dumping' is less a justification of the moral case that these countries should be helped to enjoy the same level of wages and social benefits as in the advanced countries, than a means of protecting the interests of workers and employers who already enjoy high benefits. This is morally and economically the wrong way to protect the legitimate interests of the advanced countries inside and outside the Community. Unfortunately this seems not to be accepted by M. Delors who has stated, in reply to Mrs Thatcher's Bruges speech: 'The Community has no intention of sacrificing fundamental workers' rights on the altar of economic efficiency' (Bruges, October 1989, see: *1992 The Social Dimension*, EEC, Luxembourg, 1990).

Markets work by disturbing advantages and by providing opportunities for those disadvantaged. What the attack on 'social dumping' amounts to is a demand that failing companies should be propped up and their employees locked into jobs that are disappearing as technology changes, new products emerge and old markets decline. If capital and labour are not mobile, and competition is not allowed to be the agent of propulsion, stagnation is inevitable and decline in the standard of life unavoidable.

Modern societies have for a hundred years softened the effects of economic change by social policies such as unemployment benefits and training grants which help labour and capital to move freely; but these are only legitimate if they are set at levels that can be economically funded within each member state. They will rise, as they have done, in all countries, as their economies have grown: they can only rise faster at the expense of higher taxes or subsidies from other member states, which are likely to have damaging economic and social effects.

To argue, as supporters of the Social Charter have done, in favour of creating a 'level playing field' by raising social costs in the poorer countries, funded by huge transfers from the Social Fund, is to argue against the basic principles of the Rome Treaty and the Single Market. It is to try to use the socialist method of seeking to promote equity by bureaucratic administrative means, involving protection on the one hand and cross-subsidies on the other. Using these means would require vast transfers of social funds from the more advanced countries. This raises the spectre of another financial fiasco similar to the Common Agricultural Policy, which was based on the same principles as now being advocated by supporters of the Social Charter. The results of the Social Charter would be the same as the CAP - protection of the less efficient, the slowing down of change, and almost certainly a massive degree of corruption, which has already been a feature of this type of social engineering in the Community and in socialist countries throughout the world.

Widening or deepening? The role of the Community

Since the breakdown of the Warsaw Pact and the emergence of the Eastern European states from under the tutelage of the Soviet Union with the collapse of communism, there has been a discussion of the future of the European Community as a question of widening or deepening (see B.C. Roberts, *Delors versus 1992*, Bruges Group Occasional Paper No l, 1989).

Those whose conception of the Community is of a group of independent European states combining together to create a free trade area, have emphasised the importance of widening the Community in order to establish closer links with the countries of the European Free Trade Area and former communist states such as Czechoslovakia, Hungary and Poland, and eventually the countries of the former USSR. A different view is held by the architects of the Social Charter who give priority to the merging of the member states into a unified federal state similar to the United States of America. They would do this by strengthening the central organs of the Community and extending their role, if necessary at the cost of widening the Community.

In this conflict of views over the future of the Community, the Social Charter has assumed a considerable significance, since it is seen by

M. Delors and his supporters as an essential complement to the creation of an economic and political union, thus completing steps towards the establishment of a unified state with responsibility for fiscal and monetary regulation, trade policy, foreign affairs, defence, and the welfare of its citizens through the harmonisation of social rights and benefits. This degree of centralisation will inevitably make more difficult the widening of the Community to include the many new countries on its fringe, now aspiring to become members.

At the heart of the widening or deepening conflict is the conflict of opinion within the Community over the principle of subsidiarity; that is to say, those issues which fall within the jurisdiction of the organs of the Community and those which are the exclusive responsibility of the member state. The Rome Treaty does not specifically define this dividing line, but an attempt was made to do so in the first (Luxembourg) draft revision of the Treaty considered at the Inter-Governmental Conference preparatory to Maastricht.

Article 3b of the draft Luxembourg revision states:

> The Community shall act within the limits of the powers conferred upon it by this Treaty and of the objectives assigned to it therein. In the areas which do not fall within its exclusive jurisdiction, the Community shall only take action, in accordance with the principle of subsidiarity, if and insofar as those objectives can be better achieved by the Community than by the Member States acting separately because of the scale of the effects of the proposed action.

What will be of fundamental importance in the final draft of the revision of the treaty will be the areas in which

> the Council acting by a qualified majority on a proposal from the Commission, in cooperation with the European Parliament and after consulting the Economic and Social Committee, may adopt, by means of directives, minimum requirements for gradual implementation, having regard to the conditions and technical rules obtaining in each of the Member States.

Under these somewhat ambiguous definitions the Community is called upon in the revised draft to 'support and complement Member States' activities in the following fields: health and safety, working conditions, information and consultation, equal opportunity and equal treatment, the vocational integration of persons excluded from the labour market.'

However, 'the provisions of this article shall not apply to pay, the right of association or the right to strike'. It is interesting that this revision of Article 118 of the Treaty, if put into effect, would cancel the clauses on remuneration and freedom of association in the Social Charter.

Given the support which the Commission has had from the socialist majority in the European Parliament, and from a similar majority on the Economic and Social Committee, the Commission may be tempted to pay mere lip service to the principle of subsidiarity, as it clearly has done in the opinion of employers' organisations throughout the Community, in pressing for the great extension of its role under the proposals in the Social Charter.

In the case of a difference of opinion between the Commission and the Council on the manner of voting on whether a proposal is covered by Article 118, the final decision may be determined by a reference to the European Court of Justice. The European Court not only decides jurisdictional issues; it can bypass a decision of the Council of Ministers by interpreting the Treaty on a direct application for an adjudication by a citizen or corporate body. Its decisions are not subject to appeal and have immediate binding effect on the courts of member states. The development of Community law in relation to 'equal pay for equal work', which is specified in the Treaty, was extended by the Court to the very different principle of 'equal pay for work of equal value'. It is interesting to note that in the Luxembourg draft revision of the Rome Treaty considered by the Inter-Governmental Conference the definition of equal pay as 'equal pay for male and female workers for equal work' remained unchanged, in spite of the Court's ruling.

Decisions on equal pay by the Court, especially one on sex discrimination relating to private pensions, which have been deemed equivalent to pay, have immense implications for Britain, where private pensions are much more important than in any other member state. These decisions by the Court in extending the Treaty bypass the political process by which the Treaty is amended and also the principle of subsidiarity. There is no power in the Treaty of Rome, nor in the proposals for revision by the Inter-Governmental Conference, which gives the political institutions power to nullify a Court decision by an amendment of the Treaty. In this respect there is a fundamental cleavage between the United Kingdom, which places final determination of the law in the hands of Parliament, and Continental constitutional principle which gives the ultimate decision to interpret the Treaty to the Constitutional Court.

Hence M. Delors' third reason for the Social Charter – that it would strengthen the deepening process by increasing the power of the EEC's central organs – appears well-founded, and is for that very reason a matter of great concern for those desiring a decentralised Europe which respects the principle of subsidiarity.

Harmonisation of social policies

The Commission, as represented by DG5, has long been convinced that it should aim at bringing about a uniform, trans-Community system of employment relations in place of the twelve different systems which exist. The principles of harmonisation (in Community jargon 'the approximation of laws') the Commission has adopted are based, it believes, on best practice, and are therefore legitimately imposed on member states of the community. These principles, *inter alia*, include the promotion of social dialogue; measures to increase the strength of trade unions; the development of collective bargaining at the European level, and access to information and employee participation through multi-level employee councils.

The Commission believes that the creation of a common European pattern of employee relations would have a beneficial effect on productive efficiency and, in contributing to the development of a European employment system, would help in the process of knitting the member states together. Many of its main proposals for the achievement of a uniform system were blocked by member states exercising their veto, which persuaded the Commission that it should make some concessions to the different systems by permitting them to choose between different models of, for example, systems of employee participation. Since member states were still not persuaded to accept the Commission's amendments, it set them aside until the time seemed more favourable; it has now brought them forward again as an element of the Social Charter.

The Commission has been encouraged to pursue its goal of harmonising the employment systems of the Member States by its belief that the development of multi-national enterprises is bringing about a process of increasing convergence in employment patterns. The notion that employment relations systems are converging as economic systems and standards of life converge was argued with considerable force by a group of distinguished American academics some thirty years ago (*Industrialism and Industrial Man*, Clark Kerr *et al.*, Harvard 1960.) Recently, after surveying what has actually happened during the period which has elapsed since their original study, they have come to the conclusion the forces making for differences in national employment relations systems remain extremely strong in spite of the fact that there has been a good deal of catching up in terms of economic growth (*The Future of Industrial Societies: Convergence or Continuing Diversity*? Clark Kerr, Harvard 1983.)

The theory underlying the process of economic and social convergence has a certain plausibility, in that as countries develop they tend to borrow successful methods of social administration from each other, as Britain borrowed its first system of social security from Bismark's German model, and as other countries have borrowed the British ideas of trade unionism and collective bargaining. It does not follow, however, from this interchange of social institutions that all countries in the Community are moving towards a common model; even less that the Commission has the insight to be able to spot what will turn out to be the most effective institutional arrangements for resolving employment relations problems and enforcing them on member states. It is one thing for a country to study aspects of the employment relations system of another country with a view to adopting them; this is not uncommon, but in practice it is usual for considerable modification to be made in the process of adoption. It is quite another thing for a bureaucratic body, strongly influenced by ideological predilections, to seek to impose its preferred model as generally desirable on the basis of highly dubious assumptions.

A good example of the way in which systems invented in one country and adopted in another become modified in the process can be seen from the world-wide spread of trade unionism and collective bargaining from their British origins. Examination of the employment relations systems in the USA, Canada, Australia, the former British colonies, Japan and the European countries demonstrates how local factors have greatly modified these imported institutions.

The influence of historical factors, especially political and ideological, have had a powerful and generally long-lasting influence. In most countries the response of employers and the state was at first to resist the growth of unions and collective bargaining as a danger to economic and political stability. This was followed in the democracies by limiting their power through restrictive laws, which were gradually ameliorated. The emergence of the totalitarian communist and fascist states after the First World War brought a new tactic of making union membership compulsory and incorporating them within the administrative machinery of the state.

After the Second World War, unions grew increasingly powerful in the democratic countries under legislation protecting the right to join unions, to bargain collectively and to go on strike. The exercise of these rights has created problems which in Europe have led to significantly different responses. However, in the past decade, under the influence of changing economic and political circumstances and changing social attitudes, unions have entered into a period of decline. This is a phenomenon which is occurring all over the world. Trade union membership has shrunk in France to less than 10 per cent of the employed population; in Germany to 32 per cent; in Holland to 25 per cent; in Italy to 35 per cent; in Portugal, Greece and Spain to less than 20 per cent; and in Britain from 54 per cent to 38 per cent. In the European Community only in Belgium and Denmark is membership over 70 per cent, and this is because union membership is linked to the administration of social security benefits.

Everywhere in Europe, as elsewhere in the world, union membership is substantially higher in the public than in the private sector. In the Community as a whole it is probable that less than quarter of employees in the private sector belong to unions. The strength of unions in the public sector is a reflection of the affinity of union bureaucracy with state bureaucracy, whatever the nature of the state, though especially with socialist states. The reasons for the tendency of mass organisations, such as trade unions, to enjoy a mutual relationship with socialist states, first analyzed by Robert Michels nearly a century ago, provide a persuasive explanation of the alliance which the Commission has sought to foster with the trade unions and the favourable response this has evoked from them.

The support which is being given to the Social Charter by the unions reflects the support and help which they have received from DG5 in the past and the promise the Charter offers for the future. The unions in Britain, having been exposed to the deregulation pressures of the Thatcher period, which has played some part in the decline of their membership and in reducing their bargaining power, are now looking to the social action programme to rescue them from this malaise.

From its inception British trade unions bitterly opposed the European Community as a reflection of a European social market capitalism which they distrusted. But they have increasingly begun to covet its corporatist advantages for unions as these became more evident during the Thatcher period of government. It was towards the end of the Mrs Thatcher's reign, when they began to doubt whether a Labour government would ever be re-elected, that they began to turn to the Community and to embrace what had been alien ideas. Endorsement of the Social Charter in 1990 by the TUC was the final step in the abandonment of their hostility to British membership of the Community.

It is not surprising that the employers and their organisations do not accept the efforts of the Commission to establish a uniform system of employment relations based on enhancing the power of the unions and giving them a greater role. The employers are represented in their negotiations with the Commission through a European body to which national organisations are affiliated, the Union of Industries of the European Community (UNICE), but they feel that this body exercises less influence on DG5 and the Commission than the unions exercise through their central organisation, the European Trade Union Confederation (ETUC). They have some reason for drawing this conclusion, for the Commission provides the trade unions with help and assistance through the European Trade Union Institute, and through EC-funded research bodies with their close links to DG5 and its Director of Industrial Relations.

There are also other reasons which explain why employers are strongly opposed to the harmonisation of employment relations on the basis of a compulsory model. They prefer to accommodate to their different employment relations problems by making their own adjustments, with or without union consent. Foreign-owned companies often wish to introduce managerial styles and patterns of employment relations which they believe have been a major contributor to their corporate success. Since they trade internationally, they see themselves in competition with companies in the other countries of Europe. They prefer to take advantage of differences in cost structures, specialised skills and locations which offer benefits of labour supply, production facilities and marketing. They are strongly in favour of the Community as a free-market economy, but see no benefits from the Social Charter which promises to raise their costs and to impose bureaucratic restrictions on their methods of management and corporate organisation.

There is no reason to believe that harmonisation would produce best practice in industrial relations. On the contrary, diversity of practices is likely both to be best suited to diverse industrial circumstances and to promote beneficial competition in the search for better practices.

The Commission's concept of social dialogue

The European Commission has sought to base its social policies on the basis of a dialogue between social partners. In the Rome Treaty the social dialogue was primarily to take place through the Economic and Social Committee which has only advisory status. Article 193 states: 'The Committee shall consist of representatives of various categories of economic and social activity, in particular representatives of producers, farmers, carriers, dealers, craftsmen, professional occupations and representatives of the general public.' It is surprising to note that in this list there is no mention of employers' organisations or trade unions as such. It would have been strange, given the strength and importance of these organisations, if they had not in fact been well represented on the Committee, but the Commission has gone much further than that and made them the principal representatives of producers and workers in the Community.

An important privilege enjoyed by both the employers and trade union organisations is provided by the Social Partners Bureau, attached to the office of the President of the Commission. Through this Bureau the leading officials of UNICE and the ETUC have direct access to the President and members of the Commission and their staffs. Jacques Delors sought to use the role of discussion between the representatives of the Commission, the ETUC, UNICE and CEEP (the European Centre for Public Enterprises) as a means of laying the foundations for the Commission's directives in the field of social policy. After four years of ineffective meetings at Val Duchesse in Belgium, which produced little agreement, Delors decided to go ahead independently and launched the Social Charter without the support of the employers, and with little enthusiasm from the Economic and Social Committee, which suggested that the Community should adopt the Social Charter of the Council of Europe. This suggestion was not acceptable to DG5 since it would have entailed the Commission jettisoning its directives in the social field and accepting the more flexible system of enforcement employed by the Council of Europe, which permits member states to ratify the whole, or part of, the Charter, as they think appropriate to the social needs of their citizens.

Although the unions in the Community represent a small minority of the workers, they are afforded a much more important role in the EEC's social dialogue than warranted by their membership. Together with the employers' representatives, they are members of a network of joint committees set up and serviced by the Commission, covering eight industrial sectors. They are also represented on dozens of other Community bodies. Through their links back to their national affiliates, both the UNICE and the ETUC are able to organise support for their objectives by the influence they can exert in each country on members of the Economic and Social Committee, members of the European Parliament, national governments, opposition parties and pressure groups.

Some trade unions see in the supportive activities of the Commission in the social field the possibility of emulating the trans-European mergers of business organisations. British trade union leaders have suggested such a development as a counter to the decline in union membership, as well as a means of exercising greater influence on the decision-making organs of the Community and increasing their ability to negotiate with multi-national companies at the European level. It is not known whether they have considered the possibility that this would invite the attention of the Commissioner for Competition, whose duty it is to prevent monopolies.

Following the lead given by the Social Charter, a few British union leaders are said to have had discussions with the leaders of their counterpart organisations across the Channel about the possibility of creating joint negotiating committees to engage in Euro-collective bargaining. Union efforts to persuade multi-national companies to enter into international consultative arrangements have been going on in a desultory way for the past twenty years with no success. They have recently received a fillip with the publication of a draft directive under the aegis of the Social Charter, calling for the establishment of European works councils in companies with more than one undertaking in the Community. This initiative has met with strong opposition from employers' organisations and has not been welcomed by the British government. Much publicity has been given to three or four French-based multi-nationals being prepared to hold one-day annual meetings attended by employee representatives to hear addresses by the company chairman and senior managers who give an account of the progress of the company.

These meetings could hardly be described as a significant step towards creating the type of social dialogue the promoters of the Social Charter had in mind. It is possible that more companies may be persuaded that there is some value in information meetings of this kind after 1992, but there is no evidence so far that a serious movement is taking place among employers to enter into the kind of consultative dialogue, much less collective bargaining, on the Community-wide basis the Commission and the unions would like to see. The differences in labour markets, national cultures, legal regulation and the strength of national-centred interests continue to present a formidable barrier to the emergence of Euro-unions, Euro-works committees and Euro-collective bargaining.

A fundamental criticism of the Social Charter and the concept of social dialogue is that it is the wrong model for the next century. Its basis is mass organisation and bureaucratic regulation, with the focus on Europe as the arena of consultation and collective bargaining, on the elimination of local and national diversity, and the promotion of rigid patterns of employee relations, rather than the flexibility that is the dominant theme of modern enterprise management at all levels. One of the most important reasons for the decline in union membership, as recent research has shown, is the desire of workers to be treated as individuals and to belong to small groups. Employers have become aware of the diseconomies, as well as economies, of scale; and the advantages of decentralisation over centralisation. Devolution, multi-level small groups with high degrees of responsibility and the encouragement of individual initiative and acceptance of involvement in corporate achievement are the organisational principles increasingly encouraged by today's successful business enterprises. It is evident that this type of direct relationship between worker and manager offers a greater degree of personal satisfaction than the structured systems of consultation and collective bargaining favoured by M. Delors and DG5.

Minimum wages: The Social Charter and fair remuneration

Not only, as we have seen, does the Social Charter threaten malign effects for industrial relations and increasing bureaucratic centralisation generally (the very reasons given for it revealing just how damaging the Charter would be), but it also envisages direct intervention in wages, a matter to which we now turn.

The Social Charter proclaims that: 'All employment shall be fairly remunerated.' This it further defined as: 'a decent wage shall be established particularly at the level of the basic wage'. The Charter does not specifically call for the establishment of a European minimum wage; it accepts that wage determination is a matter for the 'Member States and the two sides of industry alone'. Nonetheless, 'the Commission considers that in this field it does have a responsibility to assert its views . . . by delivering . . . an opinion'! What is more important than this disingenuous disclaimer that it does not wish to call for the setting of a European minimum wage, is that it knows this is likely to be the inevitable consequence of the Euro-bargaining system it is anxious to promote.

It is difficult to judge what exactly is 'a decent basic wage' which the Charter demands must be established. If the concept of a decent basic wage was to be set, as in the United States, as a community-wide minimum on the basis of some percentage of a national average wage across the Community, then this would give rise to a number of difficult problems. It would probably have little effect on the basic wages in the high-wage countries and therefore would have no effect on average wages, but if it significantly raised the basic rates in the low-wage countries it would also raise average wages, and this would almost certainly have a damaging effect on labour costs, social benefits and levels of unemployment.

If on the other hand the establishment of a European decent basic wage was to mean the increasing of the national minimum wage, which already exists, except in the UK, Ireland and Germany, in different forms in each member state, based upon a uniform formula but above existing levels (as anything else would not be acceptable to the trade unions), this would almost certainly raise average wage levels with possibly considerable adverse effects on unemployment and price levels.

Until a more detailed proposal is produced it is impossible to predict what effect the establishment of a Community basic wage, or the raising of member state minima, would have on the levels of demand for labour. The results of studies in the United States of the effects the national minimum wage has had on employment are diverse. The Assistant Secretary of Labor, giving evidence to the Congressional Sub-committee on Labour Standards stated:

> Research in the field of minimum wages and experience of past changes in the Fair Labor Standard Act still leaves us with considerable uncertainty regarding the impact of high minimum wages, not on the economy as a whole, but on specific groups of workers and on specific industries. In part this is because policy research has not been successful to date in separating out the effects of higher legal minimum wages from the effects of many other exogenous forces acting simultaneously on the economy.

Whatever doubts may be held on the effects of changes in the US minimum wage on low-paid workers and on the economy in general, the majority of economists in the USA believe that the evidence clearly shows that the effect on youth employment has been significantly negative.

The effects of establishing a European minimum wage at the level currently called for by British trade unions would certainly have considerably greater effects on the level of unemployment of the low paid in Britain, and also on the national economy, since an explosion in national wage levels might well result as union bargaining power is substantially greater than in the USA. This view is confirmed in the appendix to this chapter, in which Patrick Minford and Paul Ashton set out some calculations of the effect of two such illustrative proposals on the UK economy.

There are further reasons for believing that the Social Charter, if put into effect as a whole, would greatly boost labour costs in Europe, since in addition to the direct costs of the 'decent basic wage' proposal, it is necessary to take into account the costs of equalising pay and pensions; protection for part-time workers and temporary employees and for social security benefits; improvements in living and working conditions; equalising public works contracts; equalising of working time by establishing maximum durations, and restrictions on week-end work, shift work and night work; further regulation of collective redundancies; increased protection of workers' rights in bankruptcies; the right of young people to receive two years of vocational training during working hours; and numerous other proposals to come.

It is also necessary to take into account the call in the Social Charter for the establishment of the freedom of unions to negotiate collective agreements at the enterprise level, the sectoral level and at the European level, which the Charter states should be promoted. It is not clear what exactly the Commission has in mind in terms of enforcement, since it would seem unlikely, even with qualified voting, that the Council would approve a directive which would make it possible to compel employers to negotiate agreements at all these levels if they did not choose. Moreover, it has to be borne in mind that the revision of the Treaty currently under discussion proposes limitation of the power of the Community in the field of pay.

What is clear is that the proposals in the Social Charter for wages and working conditions would, if the Commission were given the power to implement them, offer a substantial potential threat to employment prospects throughout the Community and particularly in its less well-paid regions and industries.

Conclusions: there is no need for a European Social Charter

None of the reasons which have been advanced by the Directorate of Employment, Industrial Relations and Social Affairs, with the vigorous support of the President of the European Commission, make a good case for imposing on the Community a Social Charter which introduces no new principle of social protection; which creates an unnecessary additional layer of administrative bureaucracy; which is based upon an outdated ideology of uniformity and collectivist institutions; which imposes burdens on all sections of the Community, including those it is primarily intended to benefit; and which reflects a deep distrust of the free-market principles which have conquered the world and which are the foundation stones of the European Community.

The principles underlying the Charter turn the clock back to the structural functionalist doctrines which have been discredited and rejected by most of the countries which have tried to live by them. They are an attempt to return to the policies and methods of 1960s social democracy, which failed because they created organisational structures which did not satisfactorily respond to the needs of the generality of human beings. This anachronism is a folly which ought to be avoided.

There is a danger that the social dialogue approach adopted by the Commission, based on bolstering the privileges of producer organisations, will be at the expense of the great majority of consumers and individuals who are not members of these powerful groups.

The adverse effect of over-powerful unions, pointed out for over a hundred years, became unacceptably manifest in recent decades, and there have been significant changes in the law in Britain to curb the abuse of union power. It would be a costly blunder if, after the successful efforts of the Thatcher government to release Britain from the grip of the unions' anti-social activities, the outcome of the Single European Act, which owes a great deal to the determination of Mrs Thatcher to make the Community an effective free trade area, was the creation of a European trade union incubus, as a result of the social action programme initiated by the President of the European Commission.

The areas covered by the Social Charter are assumed by the Commission to have what economists term 'negative externalities', that is, an adverse influence on other member states; this is why it believes they should be harmonised. As pointed out by Victoria Curzon Price in her brilliant paper for the Institute of Economic Affairs ('Three models of European integration. Whose Europe?', *Institute of Economic Affairs*, 1989), there is no good reason in economics or social justice why, if Germany has very exacting worker-safety rules which raise production costs compared with Portugal or Spain, these two countries should be compelled to raise their worker-safety rules.

These are societal value judgements to be decided internally, at national level. Each country should remain free to decide how to allocate national income between competing objectives, for that is what worker safety legislation amounts to. The same goes for social security systems, direct taxation and the like. All these are basically consumption decisions with no spill-over effects on other countries. How and on what should the national income be spent? More safety at work? More education? More defence? There are so many claims! But it would be most presumptuous to say that they should be harmonised at the Community level.

By standing firm in resisting the proposed social chapter in the Maastricht Treaty, the British government is neither abandoning the extensive social protection which already exists in Britain, nor indicating that it will not continue to improve current standards, which are among the best in Europe, as economic and social circumstances suggest that this is desirable. It is simply properly refusing to be compelled to accept proposals which are based upon spurious principles of harmonisation, outdated ideologies, and on dangerous bureaucratic ambitions which would have adverse economic and social consequences, not only in Britain, but also in other member states.

Unfortunately the Maastricht Treaty offers little hope that it will be a step in the direction of creating a less centralised European Community. It does contain a provision which the government claims will establish the principle of subsidiarity; or as Mr. Major prefers 'minimum interference from the centre'. In fact this clause is ambiguous and even contradictory. It provides no assurance that the Commission under Jacques Delors will not seek to continue to make the provisions of the Social Charter legally binding, and in spite of the opt-out protocol that they will not be imposed upon British employers. What is required is for Parliament to refuse to ratify the Treaty and for the government to seek revisions that will effectively limit the powers of the Community to interfere in the field of employment.

Since every country in the Community is already covered by ILO conventions and could be covered if it chose by the provisions of the Social Charter of the Council of Europe, there is no valid reason why the Commission should repeat this exercise. In short, there is no need for the European Community's social action programme which violates the principles of subsidiarity. It is based on concepts of regulation which are in conflict with the principles of a free market; it places unnecessary burdens on enterprise; it does nothing to advance the long-term interest of those it is designed to protect, and it irons out cherished diversities between member states which make an important contribution to the quality and dynamic of life in Europe. In so doing it threatens the future stability and cohesion of the Community.

Appendix to Chapter 10 *Patrick Minford and Paul Ashton*

The effects in the UK of EEC wage proposals in the Social Charter

The EEC has recently published proposals in the Social Charter for raising wages to 'decent' levels throughout the EEC. Though there is some ambiguity about these proposals, it is natural to interpret them as suggesting a minimum wage; how else wages could be raised by administrative action is unclear. Various benchmarks are given at which the minimum, 'the level of decency', might be established; one such has been proposed by the Council of Europe, at 68 per cent of mean earnings of all full-time workers, male and female. It is also usually assumed that men and women are subject to the same minimum, in the spirit of equal pay legislation.

This Appendix considers the possible effect of setting a minimum wage at Council of Europe 'decency levels'. For this we have used data from the General Household Survey on the distribution of earnings, to work out the direct effect on low-paid workers' earnings. We define low-paid workers as those with wages low enough to produce a ratio of unemployment benefits to net pay of 80 per cent or more for full-time male workers. These workers are identified as being close to the 'unemployment trap': the reason for focusing on this group is made clear below. We have used the Liverpool quarterly model of the UK (for details, see Minford, Matthews and Rastogi '*A* quarterly version of the Liverpool model of the UK', Working paper No. 90/06, Liverpool Research Group in Macroeconomics) to calculate the total effects on the economy.

Our method can be illustrated on the basis that the proposal is to raise wages to 68 per cent of the mean wage for both men and women (full-time). We find that the direct effect of this would be to raise the pay of low-paid men by 21.6 per cent on average, that of women by 25.6 per cent, an overall weighted average across the low-paid affected of 24.1 per cent; this includes an allowance for part-timers.

To apply this to the Liverpool model (where wages are endogenous), we reason as follows. In order to implement a minimum wage as a result of which some people will lose their jobs (not too many it is hoped), those so unfortunate must be prevented from undercutting the minimum wage in an attempt to get back into work, illegally through the black economy. This can be achieved by paying them benefits which induce them only to offer their services at no less than the minimum wage.

This benefit support will also be seen as fair by the proposers, who intend that no-one should fall below the minimum living standard set; so if by no fault of their own people are unemployed without ability to 'price themselves back into jobs', then it is also ethical to support them. There remains the problem that some so unemployed will perhaps take the benefits and still try to work illegally below the minimum wage in the black economy. But this problem already exists and is policed by the Department of Employment fraud squad, and it is assumed to become no worse in the analysis that follows.

It is assumed therefore that the rise in the minimum wage is equivalent to a rise in benefits sufficient to raise the low-paid's wages by the direct amount estimated above, in this case 24.1 per cent overall. One could also ask what would happen if the wage was raised by this but the benefit for the unemployed was not increased. The answer must be that it would produce some violation of the minimum wage, as well as causing suffering among those made unemployed: this would reduce the impact shown here, as the minimum wage would be to some unknown degree less binding, but equally the protection of poorer people would be less effective also. So the case studied is that where the minimum wage is fully binding, because of benefit support and tight fraud inspection.

The assumption is illustrated in the Figure 10A.1.

It can be seen that the minimum-wage-cum-benefit shifts the supply curve of labour upwards, the shift at the lowest level being approximately equal to the rise in the minimum wage. As our estimate of the required rise in benefits, the extent of this shift, we use the average rise in earnings of the low-paid affected. This assumes that benefit increases can be rough-tuned to be largest for the least well paid, while being kept down for the better paid in the group.

This would occur, for example, if family men were better paid and the lowest paid were single school-leavers; the latter would get a bigger

Figure 10A.1 The labour market and minimum wages

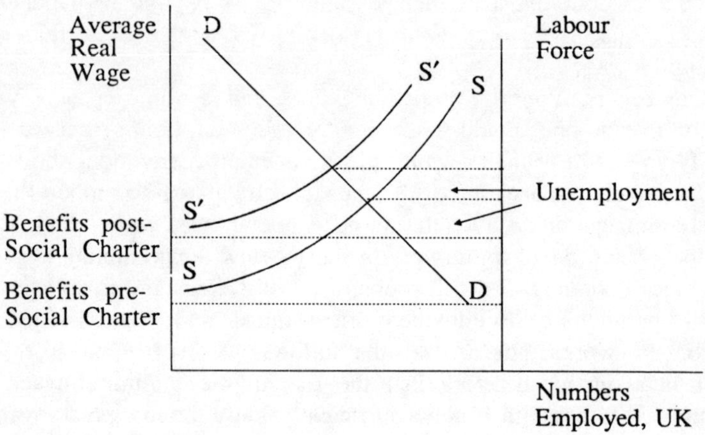

rise. If there were a poor correspondence between benefit categories and pay level, then the benefit increases needed would exceed the ones assumed here. For example, if there were low-paid family men, then family men would have to get larger benefit increases to support the minimum wage; this benefit increase would also be enjoyed by the better-off family men. To some degree, therefore, our assumption understates the required rise in benefits. But nevertheless it may not be unreasonable to suppose a degree of slippage in the system's administration as well as in the willingness to provide full benefit support. The system costed is therefore one in which the minimum wage is probably not fully binding.

To sum up, we estimate full effects on the economy by simulating within the Liverpool model a benefit rise of 24.1 per cent in the illustrated case. We show the details of our calculations for the rise in wages of the low-paid group in this case, and also in another case sometimes discussed, that where the minimum is set at 50 per cent of mean male earnings.

Table 10A.1 Effects of a Minimum Wage

Level at which minimum wage set	*Wages of low-paid group (%)*	*Change in unemployment (million)*	*Change in real wages (%, all workers)*	*GDP (%)*
50 per cent of mean male earnings	+8.1	+0.5	+4.0	-2.5
68% of mean male and female earnings	+24.1	+1.4	+11.2	-6.8

The results after three years (about the time required to reach the long-run effect) are shown in Table 10A.1.

The effect after three years on the average wages of all workers corresponding to 0.5 million unemployed (the 50 per cent case) is 4 per cent; this includes the 'knock-on' effect on other workers. The output effect is -2.5 per cent. Both wage and output effects come in rather faster than the unemployment one: wages after one year, output after two. The model's full-time profile of effects on real wages, unemployment and output is illustrated in Figures 10A.2 and 10A.3 for a 10 per cent increase in benefits (and so average wages of the low-paid group); the effects for the 50 per cent and 68 per cent cases are pro rata, respectively at 0.8 and 2.35 times those shown.

Technical details. Calculating the effects of a minimum wage on the wages of the low-paid

The methodology

Using 1980 GHS data tapes supplied by the ESRC Data Archive, we first selected our 'target group' of male and female workers whose weekly wage (or hourly equivalent for part-timers) fell below the mean average earnings of male full-time workers with replacement rates of 80 per cent or more (see discussion above). This earnings level is approximately 70 per cent of the mean average weekly earnings of all adult full-time males, or 82 per cent of full-time male and female earnings.

Our target group represents just under 50 per cent of the total GHS sample of workers, split 15/35 per cent between men and women with the same proportions for full- and part-time workers respectively; thus

Figure 10A.2 Effects of a 10% increase in the unemployment benefits on GDP and real earnings

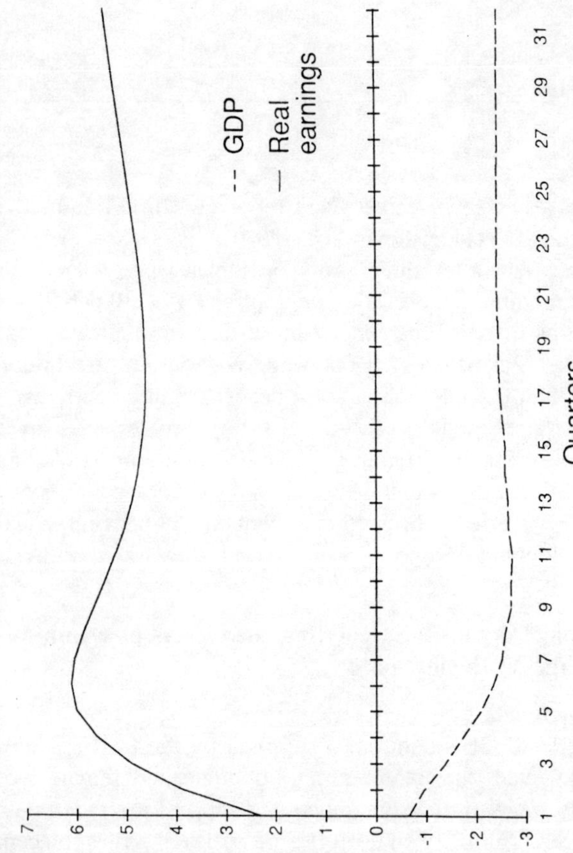

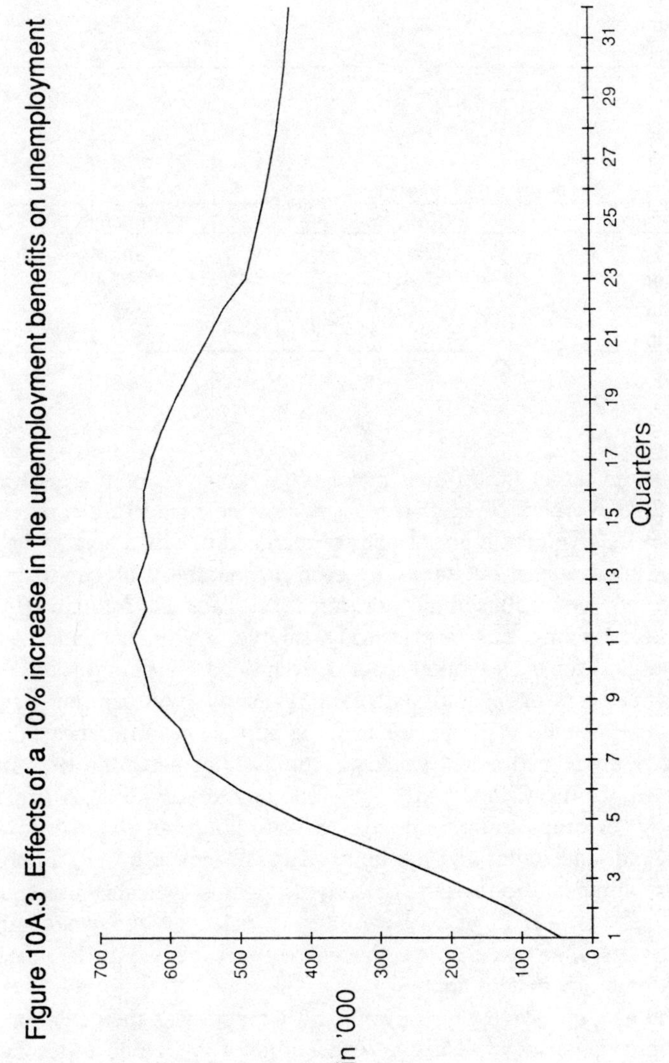

Figure 10A.3 Effects of a 10% increase in the unemployment benefits on unemployment

Table 10A.2 GHS sample of all worker

Subgroup	% of workers	% of wages bill
Men	55.5	73.1
Women	44.5	26.9
Full-timers	82.2	95.3
Part-timers	17.8	4.7

Table 10A.3 Target group of workers

Subgroup	% of workers	% of wages bill
Men	29.7	37.9
Women	70.3	62.1
Full-timers	70.2	88.0
Part-timers	29.8	12.0

within the target group men make up 30 per cent of the total as do part-time workers of both sexes (though the majority are of course women). Given the higher wages of men and of full-timers, the shares of the total wages bill taken by each are naturally higher than their respective proportions in the workforce (see Tables 10A.2 and 10A.3).

After drawing our target group sample, we then calculated the 'wage-gap' for each worker in the group whose earnings were below (a) 50 per cent of median male earnings, and (b) 68 per cent of mean male and female earnings. The wage-gap is the difference between these minima and actual weekly earnings. For part-time workers we adopted the Low Pay Unit's methodology of dividing the relevant weekly earnings minimum by 38 to obtain an hourly low-pay threshold, and multiplied the hourly pay difference by the number of hours worked. Following logically from this, we also used hourly earnings instead of weekly earnings to calculate the wage-gap for full-timers who come above the weekly threshold only by virtue of working more than 38 hours.

The average wage gap for low-paid workers was then calculated as the percentage increase in the wages bill for the group following the introduction of a minimum wage. This was, as argued above, used as our estimate of the rise in the level of unemployment benefits, to simulate the employment consequences on the whole economy.

Table 10A.4 Minimum Wage set at 50 per cent of median male earnings

Subgroup	% of target group workers affected	% rise in target group wages
All	45.5	8.1
Men	37.7	7.6
Women	48.8	8.3
Full-timers	36.2	7.2
Part-timers	67.4	14.4

Table 10A.5 Minimum wage set at 68 per cent of average earnings

Subgroup	% of target group workers affected	% rise in target group wages
All	81.3	24.1
Men	75.2	21.6
Women	83.9	25.6
Full-timers	75.0	21.9
Part-timers	96.2	39.8

The wage calculations

(a) A minimum wage at 50 per cent of median earnings. Setting the minimum wage at one half of the median average weekly earnings of male full-time adult workers, we find that 45 per cent of our target group are affected, the majority of whom (75 per cent) are women. Table 10A.4 shows the disaggregated proportions of the target group workers whose wages are raised. Comparing these figures with those in Table 10A.3, we see that although three-quarters of the those affected are women, the proportion of target group women who are affected is just under half. Similarly, while two-thirds of part-time workers in the target group are affected, as a proportion of all affected workers, part-timers account for just under half.

The total wage-gap of affected workers adds 8.1 per cent to the total wages bill of our target group. Disaggregated, we find that the wages bill for males would increase by 7.6 per cent, and for females by 8.3 per cent. This relatively small difference is largely accounted for by the use of a standard 38-hour week in calculating pay, rather than actual gross earnings including any overtime worked. For the same reason, we find a relatively large proportion of the total wage gap (68 per cent) is attributed to full-timers affected.

(b) Using the Council of Europe's so-called 'decency threshold' of 68 per cent of the mean male and female full-time earnings (which no member state has ever ratified), the number of affected workers and the size of the wage-gap would be much greater than in (a). Just over 80 per cent of the target group are designated as affected under this definition. The proportions of the target group that would be affected are given in Table 10A.5. In the affected group itself, the proportion of full-time workers increases to 65 per cent.

The wage-gap, as a proportion of the total wage bill of the target group, goes up from 8.1 per cent in (a) to 24.1 per cent under the higher minimum wage. The proportion of the total wage-gap attributed to women is two-thirds, while affected full-time workers (of both sexes) account for fully 80 per cent of the total.

11 *Tim Congdon*

Taxation in Britain and Europe in the 1990s

The questions under consideration in this chapter are twofold: 'Will Britain be the lowest-taxed nation in Europe in the late 1990s?', and 'Is it in Britain's long-term interests to accept the European Commission's plans for the harmonisation of taxes and social policy?'

The size of the state sector in Britain was reduced significantly by the Thatcher government during the 1980s. According to figures published by the OECD, the ratio of general government expenditure to GDP in the UK went down from a peak of 47.5 per cent in 1981 to 41.3 per cent in 1988. It declined further in 1989, and increased in 1990 and 1991 largely because of the effect of the recession on social security benefits. The purpose of this chapter is partly to assess whether the sustained 1980s trend towards a smaller state sector can be maintained in the 1990s. But it is also, and perhaps more importantly, to compare public spending trends in Britain and in other industrial countries, particularly in Europe.

My conclusion may be provocative. It is that in the late 1990s Britain is likely to be the lowest-taxed nation in Europe, an advantage which is largely to be attributed to the tight control over expenditure maintained during the 1980s. The Thatcherite legacy will therefore influence Britain's international financial position for many years to come. Of course, that legacy could be squandered, with much still depending on political decisions yet to be taken.

The starting-point for our discussion is to compare the relative importance of public expenditure in the main industrial countries in the 1960s and 1970s. For most of these two decades the four large European countries had a similar ratio of general government expenditure to GDP or GNP. In 1960 the figure varied from 30.1 per cent in Italy to 34.6 per cent in France, with Germany and the UK in between with

32.0 per cent and 32.6 per cent respectively. Over the next twenty years two features were apparent: a rising ratio of government spending to GDP or GNP in all countries, and a tendency for France and Italy to have slightly lower ratios than Germany and the UK.

Even so, by 1979 the differences were marginal. By then the UK had the lowest government expenditure to GDP ratio of 42.6 per cent, while France, Italy and Germany were respectively at 45.0 per cent, 45.5 per cent and 47.7 per cent. The European countries had consistently higher state spending – in relation to national income – than other large industrial countries in the Group of Seven, notably the USA and Japan.

In the 1980s, however, a marked divergence appeared between the UK and the other large European countries, and indeed between the UK and the rest of Europe as a whole. This divergence has attracted surprisingly little comment, perhaps because the statistics are not always easy to interpret. As is well known, the ratio of government spending to GDP is highly cyclical. It rises during recessions partly because the cost of certain forms of public expenditure, such as social security, increases with higher unemployment, and partly because the recession itself reduces output. But it falls during booms, as these effects go into reverse. Any assessment of trends has to be qualified by this cyclical pattern.

Thus, in the early 1980s the ratio of government spending to GDP rose very sharply in the UK, from 42.6 per cent in 1979 to 47.5 per cent in 1981. Most of this change was due to the recession in those two years, which was an unusually severe one, rather than to a fundamental failure of control. Nevertheless, some observers drew the conclusion that the Thatcher government would prove unable to curb the various pressures for ever-higher public spending. Given the vehemence of its anti-spending rhetoric, this would have been an embarrassing outcome. One of the nicer ironies of those years is that such comments may have made it easier to push through reforms which did, in the end, appreciably alter long-term trends in public expenditure. The key changes occurred in two areas: first, fiscal policy and debt control, and, second, 'social policy' broadly understood.

The effects of budgetary action, both when deficits are being reduced and when they are being increased, are self-reinforcing. The reason is that a change in the deficit or surplus affects the level of debt and, hence, the amount of debt interest in future years. Virtue receives its reward not once, but many times over. Action to cut a budget deficit now (or to raise a budget surplus) implies slower growth (or a reduction) of

Figure 11.1 The state sector in Europe, the USA and Japan – government spending as a percentage of GDP

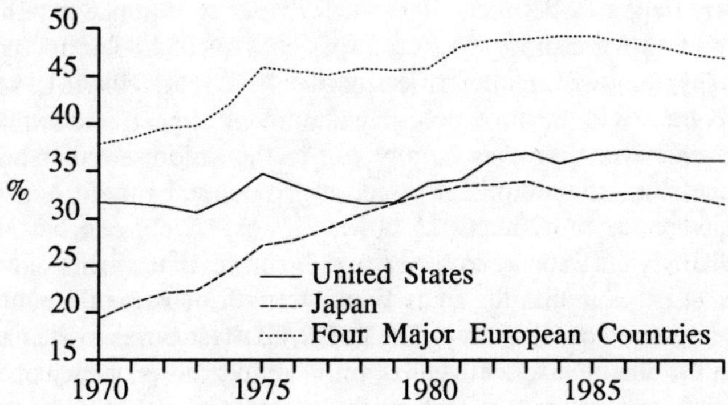

Figure 11.2 The state sector in the four large European countries – government spending as a percentage of GDP

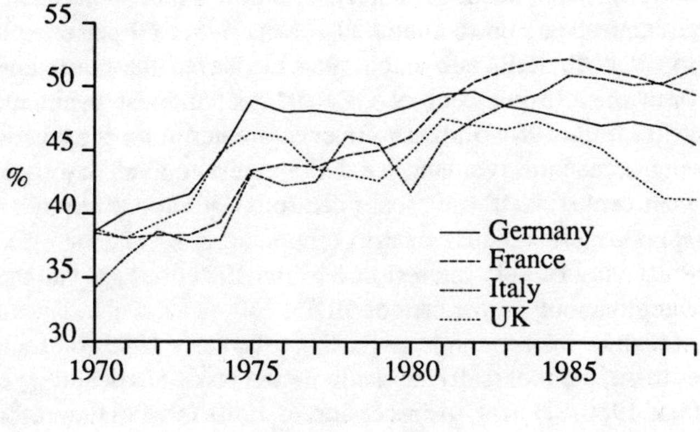

public debt in the current year, which makes possible lower debt interest charges in all years to come.

This line of argument is very important to understanding Britain's success in the 1980s in keeping public debt, and therefore debt interest costs, on a downward path. In 1980 the government announced a medium-term financial strategy (MTFS) which envisaged a reduction in the ratio of the PSBR to GDP from 3.75 per cent (or £8.5 billion) in 1980/81 to 3 per cent in 1981/82, 2 per cent in 1982/83 and 1 per cent in 1983/84. However, the target for the first year, 1980/81, was exceeded by a wide margin, with an outturn of almost £13 billion. Although the overshoot was largely due to the unforeseen harshness of the recession, it prompted a vigorous response by the government. Taxes were raised by about £5 billion, roughly 2 per cent of GDP, in the 1981 Budget in order to return to the path set in the original MTFS.

The result was that the underlying strength of Britain's public finances improved considerably. The PSBR/GDP ratio was held at about 3 per cent in the next four financial years, despite an economy operating with high unemployment and much unused capacity. Even better, as the economy returned to more normal levels of labour and capital utilisation in 1985 and 1986, the PSBR/GDP ratio dwindled to under 1 per cent and, finally, in 1987/88, the deficit was replaced by a surplus. There has subsequently been a return to significant deficit, mainly because of adverse cyclical effects. These effects should not persist in the long run.

The ratio of net public debt to GDP increased in the early years of the Thatcher government to 47.5 per cent in 1984, but then began to fall and, from 1988, declined rapidly. It is now about 30 per cent. If the average interest rate on the national debt is put at 10 per cent, the decline in the debt/GDP ratio since 1984 has saved the government the equivalent of 1.75 per cent of GDP in debt interest payments. The benefits from the 1981 Budget were even greater. It meant that over the following decade the avoidance of debt interest equivalent to approaching 25 per cent of GDP (i.e., 2 per cent of GDP multiplied by 10, plus some extra benefit because of the compounding-of-interest effect). By 1991 the saving of debt interest due to the 1981 Budget was therefore equivalent to about 2.5 per cent of GDP.

The effect of the economic setbacks of the early 1980s on social policy were also, paradoxically, to facilitate the task of expenditure control in the late 1980s. During the recession of 1980 and 1981, and for some time afterwards, most observers took a highly pessimistic view not only of the short-run outlook, but also of long-term growth prospects. For example, in its December 1982 *Economic Review* the National Institute forecast that in the 1983-87 period the average growth rate would be a meagre 1.4 per cent a year. Because of these expectations there were doubts about the economy's ability to meet pension and social security commitments over the long term. The government shared the anxiety about the growing burden of social expenditure and introduced a number of reforms which reduced its future spending obligations.

The implied cutback in the state's role of course agreed with Mrs Thatcher's own political preferences. To a lesser extent, it conformed with the attitudes of the Conservative Party as a whole. But the various changes were readily acceptable to informed commentators – and, indeed, public opinion at large – only because of the mood of pessimism and 'crisis' in the early 1980s. Because people doubted the economy's long-term ability to pay for extra public services, they were prepared to tolerate significant retrenchment of the state sector.

The reduction in the government's commitments came in two forms. First, and crucially, it became a convention that pensions, benefits and so on should be indexed to prices, not to earnings. The logic of this practice was obvious, given the general assumption in the early 1980s that the economy would suffer high unemployment and meagre 1-1.5 per cent growth into the indefinite future. However, its effect in an economy enjoying 2.5-3 per cent per year real growth in earnings – which has, in fact, been the standard performance from 1982 onwards – has been to reduce substantially the ratio to GDP of spending on the various benefits.

Indeed, if the British economy continues to grow at 2 per cent a year for another generation, the indexation of benefits to prices rather than earnings will accomplish – by itself – a veritable social revolution. 2 per cent per year growth over twenty-five years will result in a rise in national output of 85 per cent. If demographic and other influences are neutral, the effect will be virtually to halve the cost of pensions and social security as a share of GDP.

It would require considerable work to give a precise estimate of the importance of this effect over the last decade alone. But a rough indication of the order of magnitude is easy enough. In 1981 the cost of social security was £31.1 billion (according to *Social Trends*), while nominal GDP at market prices was £254.1 billion. So the ratio of social security costs to GDP was 12.75 per cent. With real incomes growing since then by 2.75 per cent a year on average, indexation to prices rather than earnings has reduced the cost of social security by 2.5-3 per cent of GDP. The ratio of social security costs to GDP has in fact fallen by about the indicated amount, being roughly 9.5 per cent in 1990/91. But this may have been partly coincidence. For example, the state-earnings related pension scheme, SERPS, was not abolished at a stroke, but only put on a course which might see it wither away over thirty or forty years. At present the cost of SERPS is still rising strongly.

Secondly, the government took various more specific measures to reduce government expenditure on pensions and social services. Perhaps the most significant were the phasing-out of SERPS and attempts to be more selective in paying benefits, notably to the unemployed. These measures were so numerous and varied that they are impossible to list in a short chapter. But their cumulative impact has undoubtedly been very great. It should also be noted that legislation to curb the power of the trade unions has helped, because it has lowered the natural rate of unemployment (i.e. the rate of unemployment associated with stable pay settlements). By reducing the sustainable level of unemployment, this has cut the public-expenditure cost of providing those out of work with a reasonable standard of living.

The combined effect of all the reforms is difficult to quantify. Much depends, in any case, on such things as the take-up of benefits and the extent to which people come to prefer private provision (of health care, insurance coverage for disablement and unemployment, etc.) over state provision. For example, there clearly has been a well-defined pattern in the last two years for private-pension provision to replace state provision, as people have opted out of SERPS and set up their own Personal Pension Plans. But initially this process has added to state expenditure, not reduced it, because of the incentives given to encourage the switch out of SERPS. Despite all the problems, it seems likely that in the medium to long term – over, say, another decade – the various changes will have lowered the share of state spending in GDP by at least 2 or 3 per cent and perhaps by over 5 per cent. (That assumes they have not been reversed by a different government.) There probably already has been some effect in this direction in the last few years.

Before we assess the outlook for the government spending to GDP ratio in coming years, one more aspect of the subject needs to be discussed. This is the influence of demography on trends in public expenditure. Demography is most relevant in three areas – education costs (which depend on the number of children and young people); the cost of state pensions (which obviously depends on the number of elderly);

and the cost of public health (which depends on the number of elderly and especially on the number of very old, i.e. over 80, whose requirements for medical attention are particularly intensive).

The key point here is that demographic trends are more or less neutral in the UK over the next twenty years. The number of elderly has been rising as a proportion of the total UK population almost continuously in the post-war period. In 1951, 5.5 million people were over 65 in a population of 50.3 million, giving a ratio of the elderly to the total of 10.9 per cent. In 1981 8.5 million were over 65 in a population of 56.4 million and the ratio of the elderly to the total was 15.1 per cent. This year there are expected to be 9.1 million over 65 in a population of 57.5 million, implying a ratio of 15.8 per cent. But that will be a peak for almost another twenty years. Official population projections are that in 2006 there will be 9.2 million elderly, constituting 15.4 per cent of a total population of 59.6 million. It is true that the ratio of old people to the total population will start rising again after 2010, but that does not present any immediate policy problem.

In qualification, it should be said that the numbers of both the very old and the young will be rising in the next fifteen years. There are projected to be 2.6 million very old people in 2006, compared with 2.2 million in 1991, while the number aged under 16 is expected to increase from 11.7 million in 1991 to 12.8 million in 2001 and 12.6 million in 2006. (The figures in this and the previous paragraph are taken from Table 1.2 in the 1991 edition of *Social Trends*.) But the extra burden of coping with these increases is modest relative to the existing costs of looking after the dependent old and young. Broadly speaking, the ratio of the working population to the total population will be stable over the next fifteen years and demography will have no adverse implications for public expenditure control.

With demography neutral in its effects, we can suggest how much the ratio of state spending to GDP will fall over the next decade if two current policies are maintained. These two policies are a balanced budget over the course of the business cycle and benefits remaining indexed to prices, not earnings. If the UK economy grew by 2.5 per cent a year and inflation was moderate, the effect of these two policies would be to reduce the share of government expenditure in GDP by about 3.5 per cent by the year 2000. With real growth of 2.5 per cent and 4 per cent inflation, the ratio of net public debt to GDP would fall from 30 per cent to 16 per cent over a decade if no new debt were issued, i.e. a balanced budget were achieved. Net debt interest would therefore fall from its present level, about 2.5 per cent of GDP, to 1 per cent of GDP. With 2 per cent real growth, i.e. almost 30 per cent in a decade, social security costs as a share of GDP, 9 per cent in 1990/91, would fall to 7 per cent by 2000/01.

The overall outcome would depend also on other kinds of public expenditure. Perhaps the most important change in prospect is a reduction in the ratio of defence spending to GDP, because of the fading of the Soviet threat to the West. Defence spending in recent years has averaged 4 per cent of GDP. It seems quite plausible that this will be reduced by 2-3 per cent of GDP in coming years. Combining this gain and the effect of ongoing trends in debt interest and social security expenditure, it is not silly to claim that in the year 2000 the ratio of government spending to GDP could be 5 per cent lower than it is at present, which would make it closer to 35 per cent than 40 per cent. Of course, the exact number would depend on the state of the business cycle and other factors. This is very much a back-of-the-envelope calculation. But the arguments which lie behind it are powerful and easy to understand, and it seems unlikely that more detailed work would lead to a very different answer.

The central conclusions of our discussion are in fact confirmed in a more academically rigorous paper in the Autumn 1990 issue of the OECD's *Economic Studies*. The paper, 'The sustainability of fiscal policy: new answers to an old question' by Olivier Blanchard, Jean-Claude Chouraqui, Robert P. Hagemann and Nicola Sartor, assesses future fiscal trends in most of the OECD countries. It confirms that the UK will have no difficulty sustaining present fiscal policies in the foreseeable future and demonstrates that prospects for public expenditure are very different in the UK from elsewhere in the OECD, particularly in the rest of Europe.

The OECD paper examines two main subjects. The first is the medium-term (i.e. five-year) correction to fiscal policy required to stabilise the ratio of net public debt to GDP or GNP. This exercise ignores all influences on the fiscal situation except the dynamics of public debt (i.e. the effect of a deficit on the future level of debt and debt interest costs, and the interaction with economic growth). The second is also concerned with the correction to fiscal policy required to stabilise the net public debt ratio, but the time-horizon is extended to forty years, and the analysis incorporates the long-term threat to expenditure control from the ageing of the population as well.

In contrast to the early 1980s, there are now relatively few countries which face medium-term fiscal difficulties. There are only two – Italy and Greece – where the problem is at all serious, although Norway, The Netherlands and Spain also need to make some adjustments. The paper estimates that, from a 1989 starting-point, Italy needed to cut the ratio of its budget deficit to GDP by 4.6 per cent and Greece by 11.1 per cent, if they wanted to stabilise their debt to GDP ratios in five years. However, its calculations also identify countries which could raise their deficit to GDP ratios without jeopardising medium-term fiscal sustainability.

It turns out that the UK could increase its deficit to GDP ratio more than any other OECD country in the next few years, without sliding into unsustainability. This is emphatically not a recommendation for so-called 'fiscal expansionism', just a comment on the underlying strength of Britain's public finances. Developments since 1989, notably various increases in public expenditure since Mrs. Thatcher's departure from office, may have undermined Britain's public finances somewhat.

But it is the long-term arithmetic which shows how impressive the UK's relative position has become. In 1990 the OECD paper estimates that non-interest government spending as a share of GNP was 33.2 per cent in the UK, somewhat higher than in the USA (31.4 per cent) and Japan (27.8 per cent), but markedly less than in the three other large European countries (40.9 per cent in Germany, 42.5 per cent in Italy and 46.8 per cent in France). Moreover, whereas the process of population ageing is more or less complete in the UK, at least until 2010, it has a long way to go in other OECD countries.

The paper therefore suggests, for the various countries, the multiples by which non-interest government spending as a share of GDP will have to increase by the year 2028 to compensate for

1. the prospective increase in pension spending taken alone; and

2. the prospective increase in spending on both pensions and health care.

The table below shows the implied ratios of non-interest spending to GDP or GNP in the Group of Seven and three smaller European countries. A striking feature is that the ratio is lower in the UK than in any other country. Indeed, it is not much more than half the level in Sweden.

Table 11.1 Non-interest government spending as a share of GDP

Table shows non-interest spending as a % of GDP, actual and predicted. Column 2 shows projections to 2028 allowing for higher pension spending only and column 3 allowing for both higher pension spending and the extra cost of health care.

	Actual 1990	Projected, 2028 (Pensions only)	Projected, 2028 (pensions and health)
USA	31.4	36.7	38.9
Japan	27.8	35.0	36.4
Germany	40.9	51.9	51.9
France	46.8	54.3	55.2
Italy	42.5	51.4	51.9
UK	33.2	35.2	35.9
Canada	33.3	38.6	41.6
Denmark	52.2	56.9	56.4
Netherlands	46.4	58.0	60.3
Sweden	54.0	61.0	62.1

Source: OECD *Economic Studies*

Even these numbers – dramatic though they are – may understate the UK's relatively favourable position, because they do not take account of a probable increase in the relative cost of health care with economic growth: the price of medical care, which is labour-intensive, rises faster than the price of other goods and services, as productivity and wages increase over time.

The OECD paper explores this aspect in a separate analysis, which widens yet further the gap between the UK and other industrial countries. As the paper remarks, when allowance is made for the tendency for health care to become more expensive, every OECD country faces a need for fiscal correction (i.e, higher taxes or spending cuts) in coming years, 'with the notable exception of the UK'.

The UK's exceptional position comes out vividly in a comparison with countries like Italy and The Netherlands, which have both a medium-term deficit problem and face significant long-term population ageing. The OECD paper shows that, assuming that the price of health care rises 2 per cent more than prices in general over the next forty years, Italy needs to raise taxes (or reduce spending) by 6.7 per cent of GDP, while The Netherlands needs to do so by 5.3 per cent, in order to stabilise the debt to GDP ratio. By contrast, the UK could cut taxes by 2.2 per cent of GDP. Since taxes are already lower in the UK than in these two other countries, the implication is that the gap in the tax burden could widen to 15 per cent or so of GDP today and still leave the UK with public finances as sound as theirs. Indeed, by early in the next century a tax differential as large as this is possible between the UK and all the other large European countries.

The purpose of referring to the OECD paper has been to show that the relatively casual observations made earlier in this paper are supported by more careful academic analysis of comparative fiscal trends. In fact, one assumption of the OECD work is misleading, but the mistake does not flatter the UK's position so much as underestimate how good it is. The OECD authors' projections of pension spending have been obtained, they say, 'by making the assumption that the ratio of public pension expenditure to GNP changes in line with variations in the old-age dependency ratio'. Implicitly, the assumption is 'that the ratio of the average pension to the average gross wage remains unchanged over time'. But we have already seen that – because of the indexing of the basic state pension to prices, not earnings – the ratio of the average state pension to the average gross wage could fall sharply in the UK in coming years. This would magnify the gap in prospective tax burdens between the UK and other European countries.

The argument presented here has many implications. First of all, it shows that – contrary to some media comment – the Thatcher government transformed the UK's international position on perhaps the most basic yardstick of a country's political orientation, the ratios of tax and state spending to national income. So far the full benefits have not come through. The tax/GDP ratio is lower in Britain than other European countries, but the difference is not all that great, largely because Britain has a smaller budget deficit than most of its neighbours. But the moderate level of the underlying deficit here, and the possibility of a return to surplus in the mid-1990s, will yield dividends later. More fundamentally, other European countries will have to raises taxes during the 1990s because of population ageing, whereas Britain will not need to do so. Indeed, as the effect of other social policy arrangements unfolds, Britain may be able to lower taxes quite sharply.

Conclusions: tax competition, not harmonisation

The central conclusion of this chapter – that tax rates will be far lower here than in other European countries by the late 1990s – seems very robust. Quite large changes in assumptions – for example, about the underlying rate of economic growth in Britain compared to elsewhere in Europe – would not affect the main point. But, of course, the whole subject is intensely political. Britain will undoubtedly have a tax advantage over the rest of Europe, but the size of that advantage will depend on a number of political decisions yet to be taken.

A debate has been brewing in the Conservative Party on these issues. In the 1991 Budget speech Mr Lamont reiterated the goal of an income tax rate of 20p in the pound, but he did nothing tangible about it. In any case his pledge was not consistent with the stable or rising expenditure to GDP ratios envisaged by the official Budget publication, the 1991/92 *Financial Statement and Budget Report* for the early 1990s. The Prime Minister has made no secret of his wish to improve the quality of public services and would presumably be prepared to pay for them by raising taxes. Mr Major's flexibility on spending and debt has also come through in his remarks in newspaper interviews that he has no 'ideological hang-ups' about budget deficits. It seems a fair generalisation that neither Mr Major nor Mr Lamont is as keen to curb the state sector in the early 1990s as Mrs Thatcher and Mr Lawson were in the 1980s.

The achievement of a significant tax advantage over the rest of Europe would be important in attracting inward investment from the USA and Japan, and in promoting a healthy economy compared with our European neighbours. However, this relative attractiveness would not be welcome to the EEC Commission in its present mode of thinking. Certain aspects of British policy might be characterised as 'social dumping', and fall foul of the Social Charter. They might also conflict with plans for tax harmonisation within the EEC, if such plans were pushed through by majority voting under a new Treaty. It would be in the interests not merely of Britain, but also of our European neighbours, if there were tax competition in Europe, not convergence towards a single European norm. Tax competition would tend to drive tax rates down and limit the size of the state sector.